G000066068

Praise for Sin_

"Single in church is an important and timely word, offering hope, freedom and practical steps in the often difficult, confusing and so often ignored reality of single life. I recommend this book to everyone – especially church leaders!"

Danielle Strickland, speaker, author, social justice advocate, Canada

"This is a provocative, challenging and much-needed book in our churches. I particularly liked the blend of biblical reflection, psychological insight and profound common sense which marks all Aukelien's speaking and writing. You will not agree with everything, but that's just the point. As Christians, we need to wrestle together with what it means to be 'single in church'."

-    *Rev. Canon Dr. Adrian Chatfield, U.K.*

"Aukelien's heart and passion for single adults is written in every word. At times I felt like she was reading my mind, understanding my own journey as a single adult and my experience in the church. So whether you are a single adult (by your choice or someone else's choice), a leader or pastor (who presently minister's to singles or would like too), this book should not only be read but studied, discussed and an action plan put into practice. A plan to better understand who the single adult is in your church, your community and even your family. A plan on how to reach, love and include them in the whole church."

-    *Kris Swiatocho, Director*
www.TheSinglesNetwork.org Ministries U.S.A.

"Single people are under-represented in church. This new book explaining some of the reasons for this, and valuably giving suggestions about how church leaders might attract and retain them, is most welcome."

-    *Dr David Pullinger FRSA, Director, Single Friendly Church*

"Single in Church is a significant resource both theologically and pastorally that will assist churches in their ministry to an often overlooked demographic. As the epidemic of loneliness impacts our society churches face a high calling and wonderful opportunity to share Christ's love. I had the joy of being Aukelien's pastor in Amsterdam. She lives and breathes what she teaches."

- *Dr. James Paton, Lead Pastor First Alliance Church, Canada*

"This book needed to be written. It dares to address one of the biggest social and relational challenges in churches - that of Christian singles and the pressure of dating and finding a life partner. It addresses the tension of trusting in the sovereignty of God and yet taking personal responsibility and showing initiative. Aukelien's refreshingly honest journey is both inspirational and full of hope. It takes super-spirituality out of the equation and replaces it with a mature spiritual insight that is both God-glorifying and also describes a journey to be enjoyed. However, this is more than a self-help manual - it offers a challenging blueprint on how church leaders can facilitate, support and interact with single people in church life. This is an issue is of vital importance - not only for excellent pastoral care but also setting culture befitting the kingdom of God and it's ongoing expansion".

- *Graham Hall, Senior Pastor Gateway Church Ashford, Kent, U.K.*

Single in Church

Myths & Possibilities

Aukelien van Abbema

Black Poodle Publishing

First published in Great Britain in 2019 by Black Poodle Publishing through Amazon Kindle

First paperback edition December 2019

Originally written in Dutch and published in Amsterdam, the Netherlands May 2012 by Ark Media
English translation by Erin van Santen-Hobbie
Cover design by Debbie Burgess @Doodlemydomain

The right of Aukelien van Abbema to be identified as the Author of the Work has been asserted by her in accordance with the Copyright, Designs and Patents Act 1988

Scripture quotes are taken from The Holy Bible, New International Version, copyright 2011 by Biblica, Inc.

www.aukelienvanabbema.nl

But there will come a time, you'll see, with no more tears.
And love will not break your heart, but dismiss your fears.
Get over your hill and see what you find there,
With grace in your heart and flowers in your hair.

After the storm - Mumford and Sons

Contents

Introduction

Our society does not often look for stories about God, but most people can't get enough of stories about love. Everyone is open to good information about educating ourselves on how we have healthy relationships, how we can have real contact, and how we can connect to each other. This is the deepest desire of every person, to be human in relation to the people around us. And if God is a God of love, of relationships and connection, it is those stories that will most show God's love and his connection with us.

When I started writing, speaking and counselling single people I was single myself. Had been for years, was for quite a few years to come as well. Speaking on singleness in churches, being single, is still one of the most scary things I've done in my life. Speaking is always daunting. It means to have courage, as Brene Brown explains so beautifully, to dare greatly. It means standing in the arena, on a platform, and trying to put into words what has touched you in your own journey of life.

For me, turning 28 and having bought my own home, doing well in a solid job and having chosen a church meant I had a settled life without the marriage and the kids I so desperately wanted. And I felt as if I had no way to find them anymore. I felt as if I had 'missed the boat'. I was too old, too settled and surely somehow not interesting enough for someone to love me. Besides, there were too many single women in church and not enough single men.

But most of all I wasn't allowed to date. The adage was to 'pray and wait'. Not to sit around and do nothing necessarily, but also not to actively pursue a dating relationship surely. If I loved God He would be enough for me. And I did. Except He wasn't. And, as far as I now know, He never intended to be.

Just as some people claim every living being is born with a God-shaped hole in their soul, I believe human beings are born with a partner-shaped hole as well. Celibacy hardly ever works, even for those dedicated to it. Being an unmarried prophet like Isaiah is not for the faint of heart. Moreover, it is hardly for anyone, only for those whom God explicitly calls and thoroughly equips.

So I went on a journey in search for a more meaningful existence as single, embracing my current relationship status, even enjoying it, while searching for a partner at the same time. It was a long journey and it brought me many highs and many lows. And although the partner is found and I'm really enjoying marriage, the destination hasn't been reached. It just has been altered. I still look for a meaningful existence, not just for me, but for my single friends, relatives and clients as well. Helping them see what I needed to learn on my journey. Helping them embrace and enjoy singleness while searching for love.

The stories singles around me tell me day to day still inspire me to keep going, to keep fighting to be the voice of a group in church that is so largely ignored. Sexual identity, marriage and parenting are all widely discussed. Stacks of books on those topics are easy to find at every Christian conference or bookshop. But meaningful input into the realm of singleness both embracing their current status and looking for another, are hard to be found.

Usually books on singleness focus on either/or. Either they praise being single and look for ways to make being single in itself a more meaningful existence, or they claim there is a perfect way to land a marriage. Now, the latter doesn't exist. There is no such thing, if there would be, no one would be single. It's hard to find a good relationship, harder even sometimes to keep a relationship good and healthy and growing. But that is what most single people want. They do not want to know how to be single, they are single, they've got that part figured out. They want to know how to date while not losing their minds over how horrible dating can be. That's why I wrote both this book and my first book, Dare to Date[1].

This book is not just for singles though. Not at all. Singleness concerns us all. When we are married now we have been single for some time in our adult life, and will be again sooner or later, or at least, half of us will. Singleness can come after divorce or after losing a spouse. Singleness can come when you are young or when you are old or somewhere in between, but chances are you will be single at some point in your life. If not, that's something to be worried about actually, but that's another topic.

I hope that this book will be enjoyed and discussed by singles as well as the people around them. Above all, I hope that the churches come to fully see and regard their single members. That leaders will see that this isn't an 'issue' to address, but a reality to acknowledge. I hope it inspires singles themselves to take their place in the communities in which they are already members.

In the end I hope leaders and single people come together to *be* the church instead of to talk about the church. So that together we, married or unmarried, can show the love of God, both inside and outside the walls of the church.

Part 1
Who is the Christian Single?

Chapter 1
Singles: facts & figures

What is a Christian single and what obstacles does he or she face? What is dating and why would anyone do it? And what is, actually, the problem with being single? There are people who are fine with being alone. They're the exception rather than the rule, but they do exist. Just as the state of being married is not a problem in itself, the state of being single is also not a problem. Just as you can be either happily or unhappily married, you can also be happily or unhappily single. Singleness can definitely have its own set of problems, but singleness in itself is not a problematic situation. It has, just as marriage does, its disadvantages, its strengths, and its pitfalls. The next chapter will be about those strengths and pitfalls.

Who is the Christian Single?
We sat in a café. Around us were tables and chairs, waiters, people greeting each other enthusiastically. People were talking animatedly at the bar. But we heard nothing, because we were having the best conversation. God, our lives, work, everything came up. At a certain moment as he spoke he took the salt and pepper shakers on the table between us and set them at the end of the table. I looked at them. I didn't ask questions, but looked

back at him. "Yes," he said with an apologetic smile, "I had the idea that it was between us." He wanted to get to know me with as few obstacles as possible in the way. I told this to a friend later. She started laughing. "Do you know what pepper and salt represent?" she said. "Um, pepper and salt?" I replied. "No," she replied. "Marriage."

It was only later that I realized the significance of that gesture. If you're on a date and get "marriage" out of the way between you and the other person, the best conversations can happen! The thought that you have to know in advance if you want to marry someone makes up the basis of checklists. The thought causes panic attacks, hindering many people from having fun and getting to know new people. First, make real contact. Get to know who is in front of you. Another single, another Christian.

The "typical Christian single" doesn't exist. Christian singles are just as diverse as Christian married people. It's a myth to think that singles are essentially different than their married fellow human beings. First, about the title 'single.' Hanneke Groenteman, a journalist, wrote about it: "By the way, what is a good alternative word for single? Alone? No, too sad. Unmarried? Too vague. Lonely? Not at all. Bachelor/ette? Sounds uncommitted. Just single, please"[2].

Someone told me yesterday about an evening her church organized for single people. Only they made a tiny mistake. They called it a night for the 'unmarried'. No one under 60 showed up. Why? People don't identify with the term unmarried, and rightly so. If you were not participating in sports officially you still don't want to be called 'unsporty' right? Maybe you stay healthy in other ways. Unmarried indicates that you are something not. Not married. It's a negative way of identifying yourself which is unnecessary. You may never marry. Being single is therefore a lot more adequate.

There *are* singles who are called to live alone for a shorter or longer time. They experience this as a calling from God, from whom they feel they have clearly heard. But these singles are the small majority. Most singles state they'd rather be in a relationship, if given the choice. It doesn't mean they are unhappy in any way, it just means that if it were completely up to them, all obstacles removed, they'd be with someone. Married, preferably.

In the western world the number of single households is rising every year. In general in Europe it's well over 50% of households that are occupied by one adult. In cities that number is even higher, varying from around 70% in cities like Amsterdam, Paris and London to 90% in Manhattan. Part of these statistics are elderly women who have lost their spouse. But a vast proportion of 20-40 year olds is single as well, about a third of them when you look at the whole of Europe[3].

It's hard to get proper statistics about the number of singles in churches. That's mainly because there is a vast difference between big city churches and small village churches. The latter will usually have a handful of single women who are either widowed or have been single all of their lives. The first will have a more diverse and bigger single audience, still with a very big gap between the number of single women versus the number of single men.

What's most notable to me though is that most of these Christian singles, even though they'd rather be married, don't seem to be searching. Because they have indicated that they expect God to provide a partner for them. My question is, how does God deal with this expectation?

God Will Give Me a Partner

I'm not the only one walking around with this question. In my search for helpful information about this subject I came across a book called *How to Get a Date Worth Keeping* by Henry Cloud, an American psychologist and theologian. He is most known for the book *Boundaries*, written with John Townsend. His approach to dating is very down-to-earth and behaviour-focused. It is something you just have to do. There are no special instructions from God, you just need to get out there and try it.

Dating is something you do, just like you do a lot of things the Bible doesn't give specific instructions on. The Bible just tells you how to be a loving, honest and mature adult in everything you do. Dating in a healthy way will form you into even more of that loving, honest and mature adult, if done well.

So how does God give you a partner when you're single? There are people who believe that God, because he can, will match them with 'the one' if that's His will. And I do believe in God's guidance. I also believe that He can guide me to my future partner. Except, how many new friends have you met because they ring the doorbell? (And if they did, how creepy would that be and how likely would it be that you become friends?) How many jobs have you had because the person who was hiring was going door to door? And how many houses have you bought this way? The only person who rings my doorbell is the delivery man if he has a package for me, or our window washer if he wants to earn a bit more money. Both seem like good guys, but I personally wouldn't want to marry either of them.

If you'd rather not be single, your goal doesn't automatically become 'to marry as quickly as possible.' This book is about dating, not marriage. Of course, each wedding begins with a first date. But the first date doesn't often lead to marriage. It just has to be one, my friends say, but as Henry Cloud says in his book, "Get a date worth keeping." Sometimes you need to kiss a lot of frogs before you find your prince.[4]

To date is to know?

Dating is an American term that is abhorred by many Christians. Why is the term often seen as a bad word? It makes them think of something cheap, of checking someone out. *Speed dating* is considered completely wrong, a meat market, a new low to which they would never sink. On the other hand, often these same people think it's okay to ask someone out for a coffee or something to eat. And because their date is wearing the wrong shoes or has weird hair, or is the wrong political party, they shrug and say, "Not my type." Not your type for what? For coffee? Is their hair or overall impression bothering you while you sip your latte?

A date doesn't necessarily lead to marriage, although every marriage starts with a date. I talk about that a lot more in my book 'Dare to Date'[5]. A date means exactly what it is: a point in time at which two people meet. An agreement to spend some time with someone else on the planet. 'Datering' is what my single church friends now call it, as in, pointing out a date on which you meet, emphasizing the date more than the meeting. Datering to have fun, to get to know the other person a little bit better. That's all.

It's not any more difficult than that, unless you make it more difficult by forcing yourself to feel The Feelings, or to Just Know. By worrying if you are or are not dating The One. By wanting to go home immediately if you sense that he or she's not The One. By thinking that dating is only about marriage.

When people say that they 'hate dating,' they often mean that it's scary. Which makes sense, because so much pressure comes with dating. Because they feel obliged to only date someone with whom they would consider a relationship, they miss out on so many amazing chances to have fun, or to get to know people that might become good friends. Or even to get to know someone who has a fantastic sibling or friend who may have the right click to start a relationship. "But I don't want to waste my time on somebody who I know won't work out," people often say. Do you really have so many other things to do? Do you really have fun plans every Thursday, Friday, or Saturday? Or are you sitting in front of another Netflix series night after night? Or are you found at the same place with the same friends making the same jokes, or (dare I say) sitting at home with your parents, once again?

Why Are You Single?

This is the question I start my dating courses with. Most singles respond to this question quite vehemently, at worst, and find it annoying, at best. "Why do you ask? Do you think *I* know why I'm still single?" Others feel accused of something, as if they are guilty. "Is it really my fault that I'm still single? It's my responsibility, right? I guess I've done something wrong." Still others feel mostly sadness. They try to avoid the sadness as much as possible, often with success, by working hard and keeping busy with friends. But as soon as any attention is paid to their single status, the feeling returns. "Actually I just really hate it. But I feel so powerless. I don't know what else I can do." That's the general answer.

As Lao-Tsé said, "A journey of 10,000 miles begins with a first step." What can you really do if you find yourself "still single" or single once again? Well, maybe absolutely nothing. Maybe you've simply had bad luck with the men or women in your life. Maybe your husband or wife died. Or you're divorced. Maybe you've never been asked out in your life. Whatever reason you now find yourself single, it could be for a very good, very understandable reason, something you had nothing to do with. But this doesn't mean that it has to remain this way. And you are also not completely powerless against your single state. Love cannot be forced, but many things leading to love can be influenced. The goal of this book is to make you aware of your thoughts and feelings when it comes to singleness.

Do you know the real reason you are single? People often list a variety of reasons. Some don't find it a problem, but the majority tends to say, "I just haven't met him/her yet." Or they indicate that they don't come across many people. Others are afraid of experiencing rejection once again. Other people talk about maybe wanting a relationship, but not enough to lose their freedom. Still others prefer to invest their time in work and friendships.

Still, there is a large group of singles secretly waiting for their prince or princess to arrive, bumping into them as if sent from heaven, like they see in movies. And when this takes too long to happen, they find themselves disappointed, giving up all hope that it will ever happen. They resign themselves to being single, and leave it there.

Singles come in an endless variety, as do the reasons why people are single. Still, it is good to be aware of the reasons and consider what plays a role in your own singleness. Not that you have to change anything; this is completely up to you. If you want to marry the perfect woman or the ideal man, be my guest. Search high and low. Or if you prefer to dedicate all your time to work, fine. Or prefer to sit at home rather than run the risk of being rejected because of those extra five pounds (which in all likelihood only you notice), be my guest. As long as you know what you're doing: choosing to stay put. And that you're, contrary to your wishes, increasing your chances of remaining single.

The Search

There are Christian singles who are in search of a partner. Where are they looking? Mainly through dating websites or apps, and in church groups, especially when there is a singles ministry ran (even though the numbers are usually so far off that it seems an unlikely place to find love). They also indicate that they are connected, and trying to get involved by going to events, seminars, or workshops. They do volunteer work in the hopes of meeting someone and also are looking for singles around their age within the church. All good options. But why does it not work for so many people?

There seems to be a popular myth that a relationship will just happen as long as you make yourself available. Singles are a market and the booths are filled with overflowing possibilities to meet someone. Dating apps and websites spring up from the ground. Parties for singles are so *now*. You can find places to speed date on the corner of every street. 'Meeting up' is the magic word. Or is this all just commercial?

A friend of mine had signed up at a dating agency, paying a few hundred euros to do so. After one date with someone who barely spoke the same language, she was told by the agency she was being picky. Another friend had paid a small fortune to acquire all the books she could find about dating. Recently someone recommended a (very expensive) dating website to me. "Money well worth it," she said, "because you get to take all kinds of personality tests. That way you know what kind of person fits you best." She is well in her forties though, and still single.

It appears that if you want to date, you need to invest some money. On the other hand, how much money are you saving if you don't marry or have children? No wedding and no larger home, no schooling, no endless amounts of nappies to buy. If you're single you're saving quite a bit. What are you willing to pay for the possibility of a relationship? A friend of mine who got married last year met her husband on a dating site. The wedding official told them that about half of the people she married today met each other the same way. That seems exceptional; according to statistics, only eight percent of couples today meet through a dating site. But what most people mention as 'meeting at a café or pub' probably counts as "got connected through an app or site, made a date to meet at a café or pub so that's what we'll call our 'how we met story'".

All of these things are lucrative; singles are a target market. But it also provides a service for many women and men. And no matter the way you first get to know each other, if you actually marry, the way you met is only a fraction of your story together. Still, for me, the call to more availability " to increase your chances" is a myth. What is often much more important is that people can take an honest look at themselves and how they relate to others.

Work on Your Life

There is a story about a man who bought an old farm surrounded by land. The land had been neglected and the farm had long been abandoned. The man began to work. He fixed up the house, making it habitable, and then started working with the land around it. After a time the fields improved. What he had sown was growing well and he anticipated a good harvest. And then the preacher stopped by. He saw the work the man was doing and said to him, "How nice that God is at work here!" to which the man replied, "You should have seen it when God was working here alone."

In Corinthians 3:7 it is written, "So neither he who plants nor he who waters is anything, but only God who gives the growth." But without planters or caretakers God cannot grow something. God does His work, but He asks us to do ours. Not to pat ourselves on the back and congratulate ourselves on how well we've done, but to point to Him and show how great He is.

Compare finding a relationship with finding a place to live. When I was twenty-eight I bought my first apartment, a significant step for anyone to take. I was single and doing post-graduate studies. In connection with the studies I wanted to move to the city. Because I was on my own, it seemed important to be able to live somewhere that had things to do and places to go in the evenings. It also seemed like fun to live within biking distance from friends. More than enough requirements. I was also faced with the fact that I was limited by my income, a nice but modest single wage-earning one. How do you find a place to live with that?

I first tried via the local rental system. You begin by applying once every two weeks for three apartments. It's then checked to see who has been waiting the longest, that person is given preference, and you are placed next on a waiting list. But before you or even those people who have waited the longest, come the people who have qualified for emergency declarations, the people who have to move because of difficult and unforeseen circumstances (i.e. renovations, medical emergencies, divorces, etc.). If you want to live in a city like Amsterdam, you have a better chance at housing if you're divorcing than if you've always been single. After months of frustration, I went to a mortgage broker.

For all of those months of waiting I had been on a estate website in order to buy an apartment, anyway. I thought that no mortgage broker would take me seriously on my own, but I was surprised when it went smoothly. Still, it seemed like an irresponsible step to take to spend so much money based upon a projected future income, without clarity about "somebody someday." What if this man appeared out of nowhere in a few months? What would I do then with the apartment? I worried about these things until someone said to me, "An apartment is not a sum of money, it's a place to feel at home, to live in, to have friends over. It's a haven." The next morning I made appointments for six viewings the following Friday, and soon the fifth apartment I viewed became *my apartment*.

This whole story about searching for a house illustrates a point about dating. What did I do to find a house? Everything. Was the search blessed? Yes. Led? I believe so. But I also worked hard on it, first carefully considering my options. I asked professionals for their advice on matters like budget, mortgage, and loan options. I took the time needed to get a clear understanding of the practical and financial big picture, while keeping my eye on the real estate website. I also quizzed friends and family about their house-buying experiences. And when the house in question was found, I was ready to go for it.

But the story goes further. The house where I was living had large storage where I kept all kinds of things, things that wouldn't fit in my new apartment. I had to sort through my belongings and get rid of a lot of things. And once I moved, I had to find a place to put everything. I had to get used to this city neighbourhood, with its different supermarket, doctor, dentist, and pharmacy. Make sure that my mail would be forwarded. And countless other small, petty things that you forget about a year later, but regardless of that cost lots of time and energy.

Meanwhile, I am still investing monthly in this house by keeping it clean and tidy (well, mostly), by paying my bills and investing in its upkeep. Does this take a lot of work, time, and money? Definitely. And is it worth it? Absolutely. It's *my* home. A place to feel safe and to live as I want to live.

Finding a relationship is a similar kind of project. It requires far more from me than just keeping my eyes open for possibilities. It requires in-depth self-examination, time investment, sometimes money, and definitely energy. It requires planning and investigating what the possibilities are. It requires going through the baggage you've acquired throughout your life. It requires hard work. And it doesn't stop with finding a relationship.

A relationship is not the final destination. Being married is not the goal. Maintaining a relationship requires constant attention and energy. There are countless other books written that can help you effortlessly in that time. An even better option is to begin reading those books now. Be prepared!

Nobody Wants to Be Alone

Singleness is sometimes called the illness of the times. We're all being too critical, too picky. We've lost track of what it is to find love and to just go for it. For many singles (both believing and not) this means we are 'serially monogamous'. In the US the average man has had eight sexual partners by the time he is twenty-two years old, and for women this average is six.[6] The numbers aren't much different in Europe, although the new generation prefers rather to abstain from sex than to have meaningless one night stands. And that makes sense. You can imagine that multiple (often fleeting) sexual relationships make an impact, despite our society's breezy treatment of sex.

Entire books are written about sex and many more can be written as well. For now I want to focus on the fact that most people don't like to be alone. People apparently need a partner, a relationship, or at least physical contact. Outside the church people are single against their wishes, and this is not different within the church. Let's not forget that God specializes in relationships. He's created us in relationship to others, as we read in Genesis 1:27: "Male and female He created them," and in Genesis 2:18, "It is not good for man to be alone, I will make a helper fit for him." But does this then mean that 'to be married' is our life goal?

In many churches single people are placed in one corner while married people are in the other, as if they're two vastly different worlds. As if relationships can be placed on a continuum, and you as an individual change when your relationship status changes. The result is often that singles feel isolated and lonely. They feel like an exception to the rule, and that hurts. This often means that they either disappear from the church or leave to find a church with more singles.

In his 1st Letter to the Corinthians, Paul writes that it is better to be alone, and this text is often used to help Christian singles make peace with their singleness. Some singles do indeed indicate that their singleness gives them time they can use well. A friend of mine told me that he's not actively searching for a relationship. He says, "I believe that the extra time I now have can be used to serve the church, so that's what I'm doing." But I also know many other singles who, because of their aloneness, invest a lot of time in work, their homes, making plans with friends and family, and dating. Their overly full calendars make them appear that they're constantly driven by a state of restlessness. This restlessness, in fact, possibly leads to less time to be able to serve the church than they might have if they were in a stable marriage.

To a church, stable marriages often provide stronger support than restless singles keeping their options open. Many singles that I know are not only looking for a relationship, but for their identity, assurance, and often also companionship. As a result, they're less committed with their schedules than the average family, choosing the option to sleep in on a Sunday morning rather than stepping into a role within their church community that requires them to show up.

"It is not good for man to be alone," yet all over the world there are millions of people living all by themselves. What does that mean for all of these people? Where do they find companionship? For many singles I know, filling up their schedules is a part-time job in and of itself. The fear of loneliness drives them into making endless dates and plans. Paul's words above surely cannot be applied to the reluctant single. In Chapter 4 I'll get further into this verse and the context of Paul's words.

Could it Be a Problem?

Someone who lives in a house full of people can long for silence, but for many singles who long for life and activity, home can be too quiet. It's understandable that they fill their diaries with dates and activities, but for many singles this can mean that they're increasingly becoming self-preoccupied, so busy are they with making their home just the way they like it, and pouring hours of work into their careers. When you're single and home alone, then often you find yourself wondering *why* you're still single. Who benefits from that line of thinking?

And who benefits from so many Christian singles believing that they have to pray and wait until God brings them a partner? What effect does that have on someone's picture of God if it appears that marriage is probably not (yet) God's plan for you? I wonder how many singles have quietly left the church, disappointed with God and/or the church. And how many singles end up with a non-believing partner?

Jesus doesn't expressly address looking for a relationship, but He does address our tendency to worry about many things when He says, "But seek first the kingdom of God and his righteousness, and all these things will be added to you. Therefore do not be anxious about tomorrow, for tomorrow will be anxious for itself" (Matthew 6:33,34). But further on in the next chapter He also says, "Ask, and it will be given to you; seek, and you will find; knock, and it will be opened to you" (Matthew 7:7). Once again a difficult dilemma for singles.

Trust in God and don't worry, but also tell God your worries and pray that your longings will be fulfilled. God gives when you ask, but sometimes He doesn't. When does He, when doesn't He, and above all, *why* or *why not*?

Another tricky verse a friend pointed my attention to this morning even, Psalm 37:4. "Delight yourself in the Lord and He will give you the desires of your heart". Is God not giving me the desire of my heart, which is to be married, because I'm not delighting in Him enough? Or is it that if and when I delight myself in Him, I'll see these desires in a different perspective? Which is it?

It's not only the Bible's ambiguity that's difficult, but as many single Christians tell me, there's another problem that goes deeper. Women complain about the lack of initiative from men, and men complain about dominant women. In her book *The Joy of Being a Woman*, Ingrid Trobisch calls this dominant behaviour in women "misplaced feminism", whereas Larry Crabb devotes an entire book to 'The silence of Adam'. Both genders come with a dynamic that is often counterproductive.

In my counselling work I see this dynamic at work all the time within relationships. She misses him and in order to feel reconnected somehow she lashes out at him. Because he doesn't respond, she feels as if she isn't strong enough in her wording. So she tries to reach him even harder, in any way she can. This is usually resulting in her being critical and what he would call 'nagging'. So he retreats, trying to save the relationship and keep the peace, so he is quiet. And this is where the tragedy happens. She mistakes his quietness for disinterest. For disconnection. For rejection even. Whereas he feels rejected already by her critical tone of voice as she tries to reach out to him. So he withdraws further as she reaches out more[7]. This is the dance couples get stuck in, but I see single people get stuck in this same dance all the time too.

As Al Hsu writes in his book *The Single Issue,*[8] singleness in of itself is not a problem, but has its own set of problems just as marriage does. You can experience singleness as problematic, just as you can experience a problematic marriage as something you want to get out of. It's therefore not the institution of marriage that's a problem, but the state of your marriage to the other person. And so it is with singleness. You may face countless problems connected to how people relate to you or how you see yourself, but singleness in itself is not the problem.

The Problems of Being Single

By now it's clear to me that being single in itself is not a problem. Yet for years I have resisted people who tried to talk to me about this very thing. I felt the opposite. Being single felt like a very big problem. I could argue that I was just as valuable as my married friends and family members, but it didn't feel that way. I felt inferior because I was not married. I had not yet arrived in the Promised Land, couldn't talk with the 'elite' who had married.

Above all, I felt like the only one who hadn't mastered this 'being single' thing, that it was my fault that I wasn't comfortable with my singleness. I tried to repress my desire to be in a relationship at the same time as trying to get into a relationship, a combination that failed. I didn't have the words to say what was bothering me, and I wasn't even able to find them in the words of books I had found about the subject.

In churches there seems to be attention paid to all types and sizes of problems within marriage, but hardly any attention given to the problems of singleness. You can walk into a Christian bookstore and find countless books on topics like communication, sexuality, and boundaries in marriage, while the books about singleness, let alone about dating or how to form a healthy relationship from the start, are seldom on bookshelves. This is a problem, because if the books aren't there, that means the words that singles need to help them in encountering the problems they face aren't there either.

The books that you will find on the shelves in these bookstores often come from the US. Which is probably good for people from the US, but even they say they don't have enough good stuff to read on these subjects. And for people in Europe it can often feel as if the difference in cultural approach is too big.

Furthermore these books seem to be divided into two distinct, polarized categories: the books aimed at those who are 'actively' searching, and the books aimed at those who are 'accepting' their status. Strangely enough, within Christian circles there are very few books to be found in the first category. And for the books that are there, the strategies of 'searching' are dubious, to say the least. Often the strategy is to do an in-depth Bible study, seek God in everything you do, until finally 'the One' shows up.[9]

You also find the second category, responding to singleness with a vague sort of acceptance, in the Christian literary scene. These books are focused on all kinds of themes, from the really practical (i.e. cooking for yourself in a one-person household), to the really emotional (i.e. dealing with loss and desire). The problem with these books is that the focus is on the unwanted situation (being single) rather than looking at the situation from different angles.

Studying an unwanted situation doesn't magically transform it into a wanted situation. Imagine that I live in a run-down house with annoying neighbours, the paint on my windowsills peeling and loud, ceaseless bickering among the neighbours. Getting into the reasons my paint is peeling or why my neighbours are fighting doesn't help me find a better home to live in. So I'm not going to research the things I don't want, but begin looking for something that I do want. If I spend my time and energy on the search instead of on the problem, the chance is greater that I'll find a place I actually want to live.

The Dating Course[10]

This book originated from a course that, for so many singles, was such a positive and hopeful experience that I was asked to put my ideas to paper. Which I did in my book Dare to Date[11]. In the end, my book contains much more than the dating course alone. What we organized in our church fitted within what our church needed at the time, and the most important thing is that we took action. We entered into conversation about the existence of singles in the church, and from that conversation this whole project began. The hope is that the conversation continues for a long time, with other churches continuing the conversation.

In the autumn of 2009 six church members (four men and two women) and myself began a thinktank about the numbers of singles in our church. Our question was, "Why are there so many singles in our church?" And "Is this a problem?" We estimated that, in that period of time, from the 2,000 weekly attenders, roughly one third were single. We asked ourselves why there was so little dating within the church, and why was it so difficult to get to know someone of the opposite sex without all kinds of expectations arising. But we began with the question: is there actually a problem?

A friend of mine recently said: 'I've heard it said that dating and marriages in the Church is a sign of LIFE. As we know, Jesus is 'the Way, the Truth and the Life' John 14:6. A Church without weddings and matches is missing out on part of this fruitful life, i.e. something's not quite right! Whereas weddings and dating is sign of health and fruit and vitality.' I love that approach.

Until we began with our project, the church leadership was in the dark about the whole 'single issue.' (Why it was such a blind spot remains a mystery.) In any regard, our initiative was welcomed with open arms and within six months the subject of singleness had our church leadership's full attention, something we were very happy with.

Our thinktank led to the organization of a course we called "The Sense and Nonsense of Dating." Henry Cloud was our guide, and his book *How to Get a Date Worth Keeping* and accompanying seminars on DVD became the basis of the course. Cloud gave us the words we had been looking for. And it began to seem that the more we dealt with the subject, the more there was to say about the subject.

As we prepared for the first course, we thought it would be difficult to get a good turnout. We had done great PR, though, with a video shown during the service, which created a nice little 'buzz' in the audience. But we hadn't anticipated 60 people signing up within an hour and a half. It's as if we had opened the floodgates! Our church seemed to be bursting with singles looking for the right words, for answers. Singles in all shapes and sizes enrolled, just as many men as women, aged twenty to fifty-nine. Since that first course, we gave courses twice a year, and there is a permanent waiting list for the next one.

I'll tell more about this course later in the book, but now it's all about the idea. What we organized is not the all-encompassing answer, the end of the search. What we offer is no quick fix: a guarantee for a partner, or a comfortable single life. But we offer something that wasn't there before, and to me that's the key. We offer a place for questions, for criticism, and encouragement where there wasn't before. Because apart from the question of why didn't somebody organize something like this sooner, it struck me that churches don't really have a way of dealing with their singles over the age of twenty-five. The 'older' group of singles seem like a forgotten group, and the feedback that I receive from this group is exactly that; they often feel forgotten and unseen. As if there's no place in the church for 'older' singles. As if you belong in the church so long as you're married by twenty-five.

The answer given to the aforementioned singles is not often, "let's create a place." Or, if there is a place created, it is usually a place to lament single life, not a place to encourage dating. But as Paige Benton[12], writer of the fascinating article 'Singled Out by God for Good' writes, "Thoreau insists that most men lead lives of quiet desperation; I insist that many singles lead lives of loud aggravation." And oh, is there ever complaining. Even if you organize something, or maybe *because* you are organizing something, you take the heat. "You can't organize a dating course. Dating is not from God," I've had one person tell me to turn around and hear another person say, "You should do a course about how to follow God's will or about personal healing, and the relationship will just happen." I also hear, often, "No men will come to these courses, or if they do, they'll all be the pathetic loser types." [13] And the ever-popular, "Just organize more social activities and the problem will be solved by itself." If you want to be praised for what you do, don't go into teaching singles dating.

35

Now people everywhere are slow to initiate things themselves and quick to burn through whatever has been organized for them. The church is no different. But many singles in the church (and outside, apparently) can act like adolescents. They eagerly take everything offered, but seem little prepared to action themselves. And married people sometimes act like the parents of the adolescents, too afraid of getting into a fight to ask critical and helpful questions. Questions that are so necessary!

What I find strange is that there is usually nothing offered within the church when it comes to the personal formation of single people. As a married couple, you can find countless material to grow as individuals as well as a couple. If you're single you lack this kind of input and challenge. In that sense, living alone can be a danger, as you're less likely to be confronted with strange habits or unhealthy ways of thinking. But in a church so much more could be looked at when it comes to the formation of singles. As Paige Benton wrote in the aforementioned article, "Yet singles, like all believers, need scriptural critique and instruction seasoned by sober grace, not condolences and putt-putt accompanied with pious platitudes."

In the last part of the book I want to get more deeply into what the church could offer. But first, I want to give you a picture of today's single.

Questions to discuss

1. We are born as individuals, but God has created us with a need for relationship. Yet we're not all experiencing a marital relationship. Which part of the responsibility is God's and which part is mine?
2. Does God have a purpose in my singleness, or do I need to find a (holy) reason for it?
3. What do you think of the story about the gardener on page 27: 'You should have seen it when God was working here alone'?
4. How do you feel about viewing dating similar to buying a house?
5. Is it ok for you to admit you don't like being alone?
6. What is the responsibility of the church when it comes to single people and their wish to be in a relationship? Is it similar to providing marriage counselling and marriage courses? Is your church taking that responsibility?

Chapter 2
Today's Single

Anna: 'I'm just a girl standing in front of a boy, asking him to love her'.

(...)

Bernie: 'But she said she wanted to go out with you?' William: 'Yeah.' Bernie: 'That's nice.' William: 'What?' Bernie: 'Well, you know, anyone saying they want to go out with you is pretty great, isn't it?'

Notting Hill – 1999, Universal Pictures International Limited

Introduction

What I love about this film I've quoted is.... so many things actually. But look at the contrast. She asks him to love her. He summarizes that as asking him out. Talk about a difference in emotional level! But this is in the end what it boils down to. Most girls just want to be loved. And most guys just want to be with someone.

This book is about the myths surrounding singleness and its possibilities. Whereas the third part of this book is more about possibilities, this section mainly deals with the myths and facts surrounding singleness.

The greatest myth seems to be the 'satisfied single', the happy single, the single who has no need to be loved apparently. Let's talk about that for a while. Other myths are the persistent myth that meeting someone 'just happens', or that 'you just have to let it go'. You hear these kind of myths repeated not only in daily conversations about singleness and dating, but also in the sermons and prayers within the church. They are spiritualized Hollywood one-liners usually. Let's see what they are really about.

More Singles Than Ever

'The typical single' doesn't exist any more than 'the typical married person' does. Singles come in all sizes and shapes, from having never been married to having married three times over but divorced, or widowed. Singlefriendlychurch.com identifies these categories[1]:

Under 30 - *People in their teens and 20s tend to consider themselves 'not yet partnered' rather than single. Nevertheless, they feel it deeply when their peers have boyfriends or girlfriends, and they do not.*

30 - 45 year olds - *This age group worries most about being single. They say they start to doubt that God has a plan for their lives, since the promise of a partner has not been fulfilled.*

46 - 60 year olds - *Single women recognise that they are now unlikely to have a family, and tend to get on with life. Many also say that through their difficulties they experience deeper* *faith. However, men do not, possibly still thinking they might meet a partner and have a family.*

Over-60s - *The over-60s appear to come to terms with their situation, worrying less about the future and being more secure in their faith. However, they feel most strongly that the church is not a good place for single people.*

These are the numbers. A third of the western population aged 16-65 is now single. These numbers are steady throughout European countries and beyond. This means 1 in 3 people considers themselves single or currently not in a steady relationship. They may be dating, but they will not be married or cohabiting. Predictions are that this number will rise up to 40 or even 50% of the population. Meanwhile bearing in mind that most single people, by far most single people, up to 98% would rather be married, provided it's a happy stable marriage (for which of course there are no guarantees).

It's striking the number of highly educated women who are single. Part of this is due to the fact that women, without a husband or children, continue their studies. Jan Latten, a population statistician at the CBS, wrote the book *Liefde à la Carte* (or *Love à la Carte*), which describes how today's women make different demands. Today's women are often highly-educated with better jobs, and therefore earning good wages. In short, the man is no longer depended on to be the solitary breadwinner, allowing women to make different demands on men. Now for many women, the man has to be an addition to their already full lives, someone to make them happy. Tough, because aren't most women secretly hoping for a guy who behaves sort of like a good girlfriend?

When a woman describes her type, how often does she say, "Strong and sensitive." (Do those two things actually go together?) "He really needs to know what he wants. He needs to live an independent life." That's what she says she wants. But going out with his friends to drink beers or watch a game, that's not what she had in mind, let alone that he asserts his independence by leaving his socks lying around.

It's not only those who have never been married who are categorized as singles, it's also the people who have been married but are now divorced. The number of single parent households is growing rapidly all over the world.

In addition, there are also blended families. Second marriages turn out to have a considerably poorer chance of success than first marriages. Third and fourth marriages have even less of a chance. In addition, living together before marriage appears to reduce the chance of the marriage being successful. All of this data explains a bit of the increase in the number of separations.[2]

Another group of people counted as single are those sixty-five and older who have lost a partner. This remains the largest percentage of singles. The question is whether they belong in a group considered 'singles.' They are living alone, but more often than not they are also searching for another partner. Love blooms eternal; even it seems, in the retirement centre.

The number of singles grows at enormous levels in the largest cities. In cities like Paris, Amsterdam, Berlin, or New York it seems as though the number of singles has surpassed the number of those living with someone else. There seems to be more choice than ever, but yet so many have not made a choice for a life partner.

Happy Single?

That the growing number of singles appears to be a social trend seems clear. But is it a problem that there are more and more people who remain single for a period? This is a good discussion. To begin with, the question is if most people experience their singleness as a problem. As earlier noted, 90% of singles are in search of a relationship. You don't begin the search for a house if you don't need one. You don't search for a partner if you don't want a partner. These 90% seemingly experience their singleness as problematic. Of all singles 75% of men and 85% of women say that they would like to marry.

According to almost all studies done on the topic, living together or being married appears to be better for the health, wealth, and happiness of both partners. According to an Australian study, a relationship decreases stress as well as reduces the chance of drug and alcohol abuse.[3] Living with someone helps you to care better for yourself. You cook more often, are healthier, and go to bed earlier. If you're sick there's someone who takes over a bit and calls the doctor. Stress is effectively counteracted by the "warm fuzzy" hormone oxytocine, where the physical proximity of the other person is important. In addition living alone carries with it the extra stress of dating, searching, and worrying about the future.

Married men seem to benefit the most in terms of health and longevity, whereas single women seem to be better off remaining single[4]. Obviously not having biological children, still one of the most dangerous things you can do as a woman, helps in this respect. Still, most of the married women I know are quite relieved to be married, and immensely happy to have children if they've been given to them. In spite of the challenges and sacrifices this brings, they prefer having a family of their own.

With being married come financial advantages as well. You can share all the costs, have the security of two incomes, and have only one household to maintain. This is a strong buffer against stress, especially in the time of crisis and unemployment. Another important buffer: married people have a larger social network. Once I heard a single sighing, "There are more and more of them. First they get married, and then it's the two of them instead of one. And then they have kids, and then there are three, four, even five. And later, when their kids marry, the family grows even more. And I will always be on my own."

In 2010 the Taiwanese Minister of Health proposed that singles pay a premium for their health insurance because they had a higher risk of psychological complaints. Fortunately for Taiwanese singles, this proposal was denied because life is already more expensive for the average single living alone. You pay more for living expenses such as grocery shopping than a cohabiting couple does. You also pay relatively more taxes. And if you want to go alone on vacation, you have to pay a similar price even for room with a single bed.

There are more expenses for a single. The endless stream of dates (that at last many singles outside the church experience), including the expenses of dinner, haircuts, make-up, and clothing. Signing up on a dating website is only made worthwhile if you pay the yearly fees. The countless wedding and baby gifts you buy but never receive also add up. On the one hand, you are saving money by not having to pay for a wedding or the costs that come with children, but on the other hand, these are the costs that can hurt the most, because in reality you would also really like to be married and have a family and you'd love to splurge on your own wedding and on baby clothes or children's books.

Finally, singles are generally less satisfied with their lives. Often it's not by much, but studies do show that singles report themselves less happy than married people. This is also a logical conclusion, when you consider the fact that you are literally wealthier and healthier within a marriage than without. There is a hopeful caveat: singles who have never been married are generally happier than those who have left a bad marriage.[5]

Hidden Loneliness

Despite the visible disadvantages, it often takes some time before singles will admit that they truly aren't satisfied with being alone. As a single you are conditioned to pretend that you are a "satisfied single." Content to be who you are, as you are. Afraid someone will throw their therapist at you the minute you admit you don't always like being single. The phrase "satisfied single," coined to weaken the sting of being alone in the world, hinders people rather than helps them. It's easier to act happier than you really are. (Especially if you run into your ex. Then it becomes particularly important to emphasize how good your life is.) Of course you don't have to be a poor, sad single, that's not what I mean. But recognising that you long for a relationship is an important part of a balanced perspective of yourself: someone who is complete, even without a partner.

In order to recognise your longings, you sometimes have to go through a grieving process. It requires courage to admit that you're longing for something in life. Complaining about this thing that's missing is something else, but it's something that most singles are more comfortable with. They complain about the lack of attention they're getting paid, or boring dates, or the lack of initiative with potential boyfriends or girlfriends. Women complain about unmotivated or indecisive men. Men complain about pushy or controlling women.

Behind all of that complaining is often a lot of pain and sadness. As a thirty-eight year old single woman wrote to me: "I'm so tired of always having to fight on my own. Moving alone, running my business alone, making plans alone. You know, I really don't want to run a business at all or be so career-focused. I'm successful at what I'm doing (and she is, for the record, highly successful), but I'd rather be a stay-at-home mom with a couple of kids." There are countless more stories like this one. The point is that people do not often look for help in dealing with their pain and sadness. They're functioning, after all. They get up every morning, take a shower, get dressed, and go to work. They don't have any diagnosable psychological problems, but they often find themselves lonely and unhappy. They are even afraid that they might be starting to go a little crazy.

Many singles try to avoid loneliness and sadness, often with success, by working hard and staying busy socially. But most people also relate to the feeling of powerlessness and hopelessness that comes with being single.

No Time to Shut Down
When do you need to begin recognising your singleness as a problem? Compare unwanted singleness with unwanted

childlessness. Of course these types of comparisons are imperfect, but the similarity of powerlessness is there with both. Infertile couples get asked about considering IVF as casually as single people can be suggested to date. As if that would solve the issues immediately. And as if they hadn't considered that!

With both situations there's also often a long period of searching for a solution, of a tension between hope and fear. The difference is that with the one there is a certain moment of knowing: it's not ever going to happen. The door is closed, and with it comes all of the grief and pain. But the beginning of the grief process can begin, even though this doesn't make it less painful.

How do you hope for what still might happen, while also mourning what not yet is? When does it become "too late" to marry? When do you begin to mourn your singleness? In addition, often as a single you are, by definition, also childless. Many singles won't allow themselves to mourn this, yet if you don't know if your partner will come "on time" (especially applicable to women), then the desire to be a parent may remain unfulfilled. This unknowing can cause a deep sadness.

A friend of mine who married for the first time at fifty-one is incredibly happy. "It's never too late," she told me. Another friend got married at forty-one, the same year as her best friend, who was forty-two. "And this happened even though there's that American statistic that you're more likely to die in a terrorist attack than to marry at this age," she told me, laughing. Still, for her not having children was a painful subject.

Apart from the desire to have children, eighteen year old girls come up to me after my workshops, to tell me that it won't happen for them. They're sure that no one will see them, no one will want them. Insecurity is, especially for single women, a huge problem. The worst of it is that women, even these young girls, see a man as the solution to their insecurities.

Often as a single, you have to explain yourself, even if you are more secure in who you are. As if you have to justify yourself, as if it's crazy that life goes on without a partner. For non-singles it also seems to appear that singles have a kind of eternal youth until they reach the same life phase of marriage and children. A friend recently told me: "At the ripe old age of thirty, I am often asked by aunts and uncles what kind of room I have. When I remind them that I own my own apartment, they seem amazed, as if home-ownership is only for the married".

It's not a question of age, because plenty of people our age (Christians or not) are married and have children. So to own a home and mortgage and the accompanying responsibilities are very normal things. Someone told me recently that even at thirty-eight her grandmother still gives her a bag of sweets every Christmas. Just like her nieces and nephews, she, "the single one", still gets Grandma's sweets, although her married-with-children brothers and sisters haven't gotten any for years now. Someone else told me she still gets seated at the childrens' table at Christmas. If you're a bachelor/ette, apparently some people still imagine you to be a child.

So it's not just on the single person who sometimes consciously or unconsciously refuses to move on in life, it's also the surrounding environment that encourages this.

Even more dangerous, sometimes your environment does more harm than good because of certain prejudices or deeply held beliefs. A friend told me that she was recently helping her sister at her one of her nieces' and nephew's birthday parties, when a neighbour watching her interact with the children was overheard saying to her sister, "You can tell she doesn't have kids." The neighbour came, saw, and disapproved. "It was mainly her tone," my friend told me later, "that made me feel totally inferior." She is also thirty years old and really longs to have her own children. But, yeah, no husband. So the subject is already a sensitive one for her. And who says that you need to have children in order to be good with them (or, for that matter, only can have children if you're good with them)? I know enough people, married or unmarried, who are fantastic with kids even though they don't have their own.

The "Market"

Women between the ages of twenty-five and thirty-five appear to be the most unhappy with their single status, statistically. The same figures about men remain unknown. Overall it appears that, until the age of twenty-five, most people find it relatively easy to meet a partner, and therefore at that age experience their singleness as less of a problem. It's a phase of life where it's normal to continually meet new people, purely because your life is geared toward meeting new people and doing new things. You're studying at university or in grad school, in an internship, still associating with university friends, or are able to go out regularly. You are able to 'automatically' meet tons of new people.

After twenty-five, something substantial changes. You begin to settle down. You get your first job, have a set group of friends, and this group more or less remains the same people. People settle down, marry, have kids, and before you know ten years have passed and your group of friends only include a few new people. This is healthy. You can't remain an adolescent, and it wouldn't fit in with your new phase of life. But if you want to get married after you turn twenty-five, then you might have a small problem.

In my practice, I work a lot with solution-oriented therapy. This kind of therapy maintains that a problem only exists if there are possible solutions. If the possibilities are not there, then you are working with a disability, not with a problem. For the overwhelming majority of these singles (with 98% being married at some point in their lives, according to statistics), a relationship will come sooner or later. Their problem of singleness is then "solved," in a manner of speaking. So singleness is not the disability people often treat it as. It's a problem. It can be solved after all by marrying. Or can it?

The striking thing is, as mentioned earlier, the 'solution' for the growing number of singles seems almost unilaterally aimed at increasing their chances of search options. Speed dating, online dating sites, and singles events seem purely intended to offer singles more networking possibilities. You just have to turn on the radio or TV and suddenly there's an advertisement for a dating site. Many internet sites have dating advertising, and all over the news is about how so-and-so is dating, but so-and-so is still single.

The dating market is a booming one, involving a lot of money. Until about twenty years ago, internet dating didn't play a role in the dating world. When it was discovered, it was deemed by many only for losers. If you were really desperate, maybe the "meat market" was something for you, but otherwise... Since then at least 8 percent of singles have found his or her partner via a dating website, and this percentage continues to increase, although it appears that you still have a better chance of meeting someone by going out or by going on vacation. Before online dating half of couples met each other in one of these two ways, and now the figure is at 35 percent or over.

Other places where people meet are at work, in the church, in sports clubs, or through friends. The average age of the 8% of people who met their partner through a dating site is thirty-five. Apparently the older you are, the more important role the internet plays in meeting new people. Statistics show that older people more often search online for a partner. But is going online the only answer? Or is there more to be said about finding love?

Becoming The One

Let's go back to the metaphor of the housing market. Zillow or Zoopla or Funda (or whatever the housing search engine in your country is called) have countless homes for sale, one selling immediately, and the other staying on the market for years. Everyone knows that simply listing your home is not enough to ensure a sale. It's also about factors that you have no control over, like the location, the size, and the surroundings. You can't change those things. And, more importantly it's about improving things that you *do* have influence over. Is your house appealing? Tidy, clean, and in good condition? Or is the paint peeling, details remaining unfinished, mould growing in the bathroom? Not one real estate agent will tell you that it is simply enough to put your house up for sale and expect it to immediately be sold. Their advice will be to clean it up, fix what's broken, make sure that you're offering something worth buying. Are you looking for a beautiful home to buy? Then you need to sell one first.

Why is it that the world of dating can so stubbornly offer the same solutions, over and over again? Make sure that you're 'available.' Make sure that you're going to parties, and that you have a profile set up on dating sites (at least three). If you can be found, then you'll find a relationship. When asking about the growing numbers of singles in my own church, people often said, "Organize more singles activities, like parties, seminars, small groups." This works well for a few people, but some church members gave this feedback: "I can't come. My schedule is so full, it's driving me insane. I just want someone who I can cuddle up with and watch some TV in the evenings. If I look at my calendar and see all of the plans and commitments I have, I want to cry."

The beautiful thing about the solution of 'meeting more people' gives you the excuse that the reason why you're single has nothing to do with you. You're meeting people, but apparently not the right ones; simple, right? What you *can* do is meet even *more* people, get out even *more*. That way we can ignore the other factors, such as the way you date, your views on relationships and expectations, or the influence of the disappointing experiences you've had. You ignore the paint that's chipping off, the way you're not taking care of yourself, we don't need to talk about that. No need to address the broken things, the past mistakes made in your youth, we'll keep that to ourselves. To what extent are you trying to find "the One" in the hopes that he or she will solve all of your problems, instead of becoming "the One" for someone else?

Difficulty in Choosing

Recently I watched a documentary on women wanting to freeze their eggs, because they hadn't found The One yet. One of the women interviewed hadn't had a boyfriend for five years. She blamed it on bad luck. Not at word about her own responsibility in the matter. She felt stuck, powerless, on one hand the biological clock was ticking while on the other she kept rejecting possible fathers to her wanted children. In one scene her father tells her, in a hushed tone of voice, almost apologetically something along the lines of "you want to do everything yourself, so where's the place for a man in your life?" whereupon he is immediately thrown out of the kitchen by her mom. But he made a very fair point! If you want a partner and a kid, how will you make space for both and will they be allowed their own space and opinions or not?

Our networks are growing. Virtually, at least. We meet more and more "friends," possible-friends, and acquaintances. Where your network was previously limited to family and neighbourhood, thanks to social media your reach is now greater than ever. Psychologists are seriously asking themselves what kind of consequences this has on the quality of our relationships. Opinions are divided, but are increasingly going in the direction that social media is beneficial to our relationships, as it increases an overall "sociability." Recent research also points to out that online social interaction increases our brain activity. If a greater social network could be a solution, then we should have fewer problems than ever before at finding the right partner.

You might wonder if we have too much choice. Recent research on the effectiveness of speed dating shows that more choice doesn't necessarily lead to better choices. In fact, it's precisely the abundance of choices that can be paralyzing. I was in the States on vacation with friends who took me to a supermarket. "And this isn't even the biggest one," they warned me. One thing that stood out to me was the cereal aisle: organic, with sugar, without sugar, with extra vitamins, with all sorts of grains, etc. Once I arrived back home I was so happy with my little supermarket with three choices max per product. My life is already complex enough.

We can now date people from all over the world. Dating apps and websites make them 'available' to us. But does that really help? Or do we have too many choices? Choosing to late, leaving it too long? Wanting to make the perfect choice, given all the options?

Commitment phobia

'Commitment phobia' means the fear of attaching to someone just as much as it means being afraid to enter into an intimate relationship. Usually the fear of being abandoned is related. The word didn't exist a hundred years ago, not because attachment anxiety didn't exists, but because not attaching wasn't an option. You got married, period. More out of an economic necessity than from love. Romance was often a luxury that most could not afford. It was nice if you developed feelings for your partner, but it often did not begin that way.

A friend of mine was dating a guy for a while who she began to like more and more. Everyone around them thought that they were a good match. They had the same educational background, held good jobs, and were involved in their church. They had good conversations and a lot of fun together. He made her laugh and she respected how he lived his life.

But she felt him hesitating. At one point the 'define the relationship' talk happened, where they talked about where this was going. He admitted that he liked her, but he didn't know if he could feel more for her than he did. She didn't feel as if they needed to decide then and there, so she asked him out again. He agreed that it would be fun. He forgot about the date as soon as she was gone, but she went away dreaming of the two of them as a couple. After a while he called her, they had fun, made plans, until the subject circled back to where they were at together. No, his feelings still weren't very strong, he admitted. But her feelings were so strong for him, because in her mind they were already half engaged!

That's when they parted ways. Really? He was thirty, had never had a girlfriend, and was more rational than emotional. If he didn't feel something now, then he was never going to feel something. She had had this situation over and over again and allowed herself to dream much further than reality gave her reason to.

To uncover his feelings in this part is tricky. In our culture, the only reason it seems possible to start a relationship with someone is if you feel 'it.' The click, the spark, the electricity flowing through your veins. No feeling means no relationship, you either feel it or you don't. Even if someone fits you like a glove, falling in love is the key to connection. Or so we say.

There is, of course, something to this. To enter into a relationship with someone else, you do need a certain level of attraction. A driving force is needed to pull you from your place of safety and open your heart. Falling in love does this. To find the motivation to keep dating someone, to put your best foot forward for someone else, infatuation is very important. But is it necessary? Is it a condition? What if the [attraction/infatuation/love] isn't there, although the match looks great on paper?

The friend who told me this story asked me what I would have done. Leave it alone? Or tell the truth? But what decides what is or isn't the truth? My opinion in her story was that she wanted a little too much and he was a little too scared, and that they were reinforcing each other in this dynamic. The more she wanted, the more he felt as though he needed to run in the other direction. The more afraid he became, the less he was able to feel, and the stronger her tendency became to go after him.

She could have told him that he shouldn't have led her on like that, that if he kept doing things this way he would never have a girlfriend, or that dating someone can also mean that one or the other will fall in love. After all, wasn't that actually the point? She could have also said that he was making his choices out of a fear of commitment. That wouldn't have saved her relationship, but it would have given him some insight into himself. However unsolicited advice doesn't often go over well, so she decided to leave it be.

There is nothing wrong with a healthy dose of commitment phobia. Connecting with someone, especially when it's such an intimate connection like a relationship, is scary. There is a lot at stake. You decide to stay open, to be vulnerable, and all for someone you don't know that well. In that way, it's good not just to jump in blindly. If there was no such thing as a fear of commitment, there would be far more destructive relationships. A healthy fear of commitment can protect you from impulsive actions. Problem is, most people base their decision on too little information. They decide the click or the feelings are not there, so they stop getting to know the person.

What is a healthy dose of fear and when does fear become a true commitment phobia? It is really easy to say that someone has commitment phobia, but much harder to measure if the fear that someone is dealing with is unhealthy. It becomes unhealthy when he or she is actually hindered from entering into any relationship.

A friend told me how his therapist had pointed out to him the fact that his fear of commitment could also mean a deep desire to connect. You don't have to be afraid of something that doesn't touch you, interest you, or absorb you, his coach said. The very fact that you're hesitating to ask your girlfriend to marry you actually indicates that you really value your connection with her. Backing off at the same time, makes sense. You can't just make big decisions in an instant, they take time and focus. And if you didn't have the wish to connect you wouldn't have ended up in this situation.

Requirements, Wishes, and Type

Everyone is in search of his or her 'type,' and sets certain 'requirements' for this type. If you ask the average thirty-year-old single to make a list of requirements that a potential partner might have, then the list will probably comprise ten to fifteen requirements. The list seems to grow along with the years.

The requirements can vary from essential to hilarious to even tragic. Essential requirements can be, for example, "he has to be trustworthy, attentive" or "she has to be independent from her parents, have her own opinion about things." Here it's about fundamental character traits and maturity. Whole books have been written about what the requirements should be for the qualities you seek in a partner. Some of the books make a good point, others not so much.

You'll find unrealistic requirements in all shapes and sizes. I read this morning in The Times that Marcel, age 34, really wanted a woman who knew what she wanted, had sex appeal, was elegant, and possessed a lust for life (whatever he meant by that). But she also had to be able to support his life as an athlete, someone who went to bed early and ate healthily. What was she then supposed to do with her sex appeal or lust for life if he kept going to bed early? I asked myself when I read this.

Another list was from a friend of mine, 35, who was looking for a man with a heart for God and a passion for the mission field. He had to have been raised in the church and have gone all of his life. He also had to be interculturally aware and preferably from another country. She couldn't find this man, or if she did, he was unfortunately already married. She's since gotten married to an ethnocentric guy who happened to live in the same city. With a big heart for God, though.

The requirements people make are very often close to the tragic. The tragedy is that the sheer length of many of these lists, or what they mean, keep people from finding the 'ideal' person. It's too difficult. Often the lists grow along with the years. You've gone out for a while with someone with awful shoes and you've decided that you really cannot continue to look at them. Or, even more essential, you've been dumped by someone with a true commitment phobia and see every hesitation of the man you're currently dating as a sign of commitment phobia.

Requirements originate from longings and desires. You long to be connected to someone, so you give a "requirement" for the person in question until you know that connection is capable of happening. Behind every requirement on every wish list is usually something good, a sincere desire. The question is then how to formulate your desire in that way. If I desire, for example, a man who takes good care of his appearance and dresses well, then I my list of requirements might include something like, "someone who doesn't wear sneakers unless he is working out." But my *desire* is for someone who dresses nicely and cares about his appearance.

Many of the men around me say that they'd like to meet a woman who is independent and driven. She doesn't necessarily need to have her own start-up, but what these men are longing for is a woman who can stand tall next to them. A woman who knows how to enjoy herself when he is out with friends. A woman who dares to give her own opinion, even when it's different from his own. So he's not making unreasonable demands; what he is doing is expressing a longing for a partnership as equals. My friend, the one who told me about her requirement that her future husband would be a missionary who dedicated his life radically to God, was really saying that she longed for someone with whom she could serve God with. When she met her husband, it became apparent that the way in which they did this wasn't as important. Serving God together could 'just' be in their own country.

Timothy Keller is a pastor in New York City. In 1991 he preached a wonderful series on marriage that was compiled into the book, *The Meaning of Marriage.* This book is an absolute must-read for singles as well as married Christians. Keller explains that commitment phobia is something from our time. The fear of commitment is the fear of connecting with someone who isn't perfect. Or, as Keller says, what the modern world says is this: keep all your options open! Never let yourself be limited or vulnerable to anyone in any way. If you must marry, make sure it's a flexible arrangement. And yet marriage is intended to be the securest form of connection that you can enter into in your lifetime. The only relationship that you know is until "death do you part." That's precisely the strength of marriage, says Keller. Terrifying? Yes. But then again, life usually is. Worth the effort? Absolutely!

Believing in 'The One'

Our expectations are strongly coloured by Hollywood, resulting in forming the unconscious expectations of women especially. We expect that marriage will be an endless state of happiness, that we'll always be understood and known. We expect to meet 'The One.' In the course I give I sometimes invite a married couple to explore (or explode) some marriage myths (styled after the TV programme, MythBusters). The truth is revealed based upon ten myths about marriage, myths like "I'll always be in love," or "When I'm married my life really begins," or "my partner completes me." For an hour and a half, fifty singles are hanging on the couple's every word. These are things some of them have never heard.

We tend to think that love is all flowers, rainbows, unicorns and butterflies, with the accompanying violin music and the blissful feeling that you "just know." If it's possible in the movies, it must be possible in real life. Being in love is a definite requirement and condition of this kind of love, even though the truth is that being in love (or infatuation) is a chemical state-of-being that, by definition, is finite. What we call 'love' in the movies is in fact just lust and body chemistry.

Research shows that infatuation has the same effect on the brain as cocaine. It causes partners to overestimate one another's potential and gives way to idealisation. We become unable to see the differences, or we see them but don't attach any value to them. If you decide to be together based upon a feeling, completely without your rational mind or asking the opinions of others who know you well, or without having spent a lot of time with the other person, then you're making a dangerous choice. Because one day you could wake up thinking that you are waking up next to the 'Wrong One.' A day when the effects of infatuation have finally faded away.

The danger may even be greater for us as Christians. The conviction of saving sex for marriage seems to be at odds with the effect of falling in love. It's exactly when you are in love, that the desire for sex seems overwhelming. I know a few very young couples that within a year of falling in love decided to marry. For them, living together wasn't an option. Many times these young couples are just fine when the infatuation is gone, and learn to live with each other without it, but this isn't always the case. Personally, I am a proponent of waiting for sex until marriage. But if 'no sex before marriage' leads to marrying too quickly based upon romantic ideals, the most important purpose of marriage gets overlooked. Infatuation transforms everyone into 'the One.'

Actually 'the One' doesn't exist. This is the way I start most courses and workshops: The one doesn't exist. Forget about it. Stop looking for 'the One' because you won't find him or her. So relax, sit back, and listen to what I'm teaching you here, and stop looking around to see if 'The One' might be here. There is only one One, and that is Jesus. He's the only one who will complete you perfectly, who always understands you, and in all circumstances loves you unconditionally. It's also worth noting that your feelings aren't always true, you don't always understand yourself, and you certainly don't always love yourself. How can you expect someone else to?

The idea of 'the One' is also not biblical. The idea that there is a special person designated by God for everyone, is a deeply selfish one. It is me-focused, as in, "How do I get what's best for *me*?" God didn't create others to complete me. That is an idea with roots in Greek mythology. Marrying isn't a matter of choosing the right one, but of doing the right things[6].

Stopping the search for 'the One' can be an enormous relief. If the perfect partner doesn't exist, then suddenly there are so many more options! Of course searching for a good match is a good idea, for someone you share values with and enjoy being with. But the match never needs to be perfect. In Keller's book *The Meaning of Marriage*, he writes reminding his readers to first make sure you are friends. Friendship is the best foundation for a marriage. A deeply rooted friendship can continue nourishing love, while infatuation cannot.

Working on Your Relationship

In *Psychology Today* New York therapist Ken Page wrote, 'We have been given a binary model to work with, good or bad, accept or leave. We haven't been given any tools to work on relationships, to improve them or adjust them (paraphrasing mine)'[7]. This is why we keep looking for 'the One.' If you expect an immediate 'oneness' between you and your partner, then you better make sure you've chosen the best possible partner. On the other hand, if you know that a relationship can always be tinkered with, worked on, and that marriage provides a context in which to grow closer, then the need to search for 'the One' lessens.

In my line of work I speak with many couples with marriage issues, issues that often are about the same thing: expectations. My husband is not who I expected him to be. My wife doesn't meet the idea I had of a wife. He or she doesn't complete me, doesn't often understand me, or actually even like me. Welcome to the broken world! Don't wait until the other person "gets" you, but learn to express what *you* need, I (and all the other therapists around the world) say. Find a place to be and really talk to each other. Explain how something comes across to you, how you react to things, and how you work until the other person understands more of how you tick, and vice versa. And tell them what you need.

This is an art form that requires a lot of practice. Singles that date expecting someone to 'automatically' understand them will be disappointed. What they have to learn even in the process of dating is to be responsible for expressing what they feel and what they need to the other person. Lately this guy wanted to date my friend. This man (who will remain anonymous) in his own words, lives 'by the seat of his pants.' Which resulted in his being unable to plan for a date Saturday as soon as Tuesday. Fine for him, but my friend likes to know how to plan and enjoys living according to schedule. She needs clarity about what time they would meet up earlier in the week, instead of on the day itself. That's just not her style, and that's also fine. But she had not communicated that need, which means that he did not meet it. Instead, she told him on the date itself. She was no longer ready to wait for more clarity until he was ready, and actually she also couldn't blame him until she had told him how she felt.

Dating helps you practise your relationship skills. That's why dating is hardly ever 'a waste,' even if it turns out you're not compatible. You can already invest in your future marriage in the manner in which you date. After all, you're learning to communicate with someone who is another gender and is teaching you to own what you feel and to express it.

Happiness is Attainable

"That's well and good, but I just have had really crappy experiences with dating," people tell me regularly. "I've been hurt pretty badly. I just don't want to date anymore, the risk is too great. So what should I do?" As C.S. Lewis writes, "Love anything and your heart will be wrung and possibly broken. If you want to make sure of keeping it intact you must give it to no one, not even an animal. Wrap it carefully round with hobbies and little luxuries; avoid all entanglements. Lock it up safe in the casket or coffin of your selfishness. But in that casket, safe, dark, motionless, airless, it will change. It will not be broken; it will become unbreakable, impenetrable, irredeemable. To love is to be vulnerable."[8]

In other words, yes. When it comes to relationships, whatever the kind, hurt is a possibility. That is life. In our society, happiness feels like the norm, and we expect it to be attainable. There is so little room for pain or sadness that we hardly know how to deal with it when it comes. That's when counselling comes in. Therapy is my profession and I will always defend the importance therapists, but I still think that there is so little room for life's questions and "normal" pain in daily life. For these things you're supposed to go to counselling.

Take grieving, for example. Grieving is a natural reaction to the loss of something like a job or a home, as well as someone you love. It's a very healthy and necessary sadness. You must be able to experience and feel the pain in order to be able to continue really living. Loss is always painful, but so is the reality of a broken world. In his book *Connecting,* Larry Crabb argues for more church communities where there is more room for grieving so that the need for counselling is less. The kind of community, he says, that offers care for those carrying the weight of life's difficult questions. This would mean that someone with such questions wouldn't have to go to a counsellor directly, as is so often the case now, but would be able to share them in the safety of his or her community.

The pressure to be happy is everywhere. Open the pages of most magazines and you see immediately, I have to feel good and happy, otherwise something in me (or in my life) is fundamentally wrong. A friend of mine told me that she stopped reading women's magazines at seventeen. She said, "I was pretty confident. Still, I noticed that each time I cracked open one of those magazines, I felt off. As if a door for comparison was opened: which one of us was happier, which of us was more satisfied with life? Unconsciously I began to feel as though I myself wasn't that interesting, and I felt that sneaking up on me every time."

One look at Facebook or Instagram and this is further confirmed: everyone is happy except for me. We quickly forget that most people often post the best and brightest moments, the fun parties or the best pictures. Who doesn't recognise the uncomfortable feeling of looking on Instagram and feeling paled in comparison to everybody else's happy life? Everybody else is having so much fun. They have amazing, fulfilling jobs. What if no one likes my status update? And what do I have to post on Facebook? Social media may help you become more social, but it can also help you become more unhappy.

Part of our dating course is about 'dating yourself,' facing your own trials head on, in order to become a more inviting person (to yourself as well as others). The goal is not to be perfectly happy. In Parker Palmer's book *A Hidden Wholeness*, he says that wholeness does not mean perfection, but that embracing brokenness is a part of life. So happiness is not to experience perfect happiness, but to accept the brokenness. Your goal then is not to become perfectly happy, but to live your life as it is now, single or married.

Sexuality

Something else our society expects of us is to be sexually active. We receive two extremely conflicting messages concerning sexuality: On the one hand, sex is special and mind-blowing, while at the same time freely available and a universal right for everyone. Sex is a given. On the other hand, the church seems to send the message: No sex allowed, at least until you're married. In the meantime we're aware that many within the church are making their own sexual choices outside of this message. But what are all of those singles twenty-five and older to do with their sexuality?

My non-Christian friends can't even comprehend why I choose for sexual purity. For me this means waiting to have sex until I've married the person I want to spend the rest of my life with[9]. In their world this is inconceivable, outdated, and repressive. Which is exactly how it feels, sometimes. Even though I stand behind my convictions 100 percent, it's not an easy choice to make. In our society choosing not to have sex means that you are a sexless person, and being sexless is out of the question.

What's beautiful is that God created sexuality as part of our identity. It's much more than the choice to have sex or not have sex. In his book *Sex God*, Rob Bell wrote how God designed sexuality. A friend of mine is in his 30's, single and choosing a celibate life. What is so powerful about his life and work is how openly he speaks about his sexuality and how he uses this energy to connect, in a nonsexual way. To make friends, to have community right where he is. If you see your sexual energy as a creative and connective energy, Bell says, then you come to a broader definition of sexuality. What he means is that sexuality is the kind of energy you can use to connect with all kinds of people, or making your existing relationships stronger.

Which means that sexuality is not just about if you're sexually active or not. Sexuality is not about your sexual behaviours but is more about the core of your identity. Single people in church tend to either be controlled by their sexuality or to completely suppress their sexuality, both men and women.

The one extreme means jumping into bed on every date. People having sex outside marriage, or "isolated" incidents of sex. Sex for sex's sake. It can also be less extreme. There are singles who flirt with every person they encounter. Singles who rate others based upon their looks or sex appeal. People whose "requirements" list is made up of mostly physical qualities. Maybe these singles don't go to bed with everyone, but they are still predominately guided by their sexuality. You know them: the players, the heartbreakers. The people who get their meaning, their self-esteem, from the other person.

The other extreme is never flirting, or avoiding everything related to "sexual behaviour." This is a kind of sexuality that students in my university club called, "hiding under a rock." Never dressing pretty or feminine as a woman, never taking the lead as a man. Denying wants and desires without acknowledging them. Ignoring everything to do with sexual desire, as if it doesn't even exist. That kind of sexual suppression doesn't help. Sure, it provides a level of safety, but you don't learn how to deal with the tension that comes along with your sexuality in the relationships you have.

You need both. You are a sexual human being. And sometimes someone can be a good fit in every other way but you don't feel at all physically drawn to them. That's not something to ignore. Just don't lead with your sexuality. Also, don't repress it. The world is missing out on part of you if you act as if you are asexual altogether. You are not. Find your inner flirt.

For a healthy balance you need an appropriate awareness of your sexual identity. This can mean that it's possible for you to choose against having sex (for now). Just as brokenness can be a good teacher in our craving for perfection, so can the self-control we need to postpone our sexual desires. In the end, it helps us have a much more satisfying experience. Learning to deal with your sexuality as a single can reap benefits for your life as a married person. After all, you can't always respond to every sexual desire you have. Even then, your sexuality must be an integrated part of who you are.

Marrying Now

If you want to learn about singleness and dating, you have to also learn about marriage. I believe in the power of marriage. Timothy Keller articulates it in *The Meaning of Marriage* as follows: Marriage is a powerful tool for the renewal of your heart. It changes you from the inside. It's mirroring the gospel: we are more flawed than we ever thought possible and more loved and accepted in Jesus Christ than we ever dared hope for. Keller is saying that of course hard times are a part of marriage. Working through those bad times is the key. It brings you closer together and closer to God.

'Staying Together is the New Divorce' I hear lately. In general, divorce doesn't solve anything, has been the consensus of magazines more and more lately. Financially things are tougher and emotionally, the question is if it will be everything you had hoped for in the long run. Clients with serious relationship problems often come to our practice because we have a Christian worldview. Their experience is that other therapists begin the process of divorces much sooner. It is rarely our job to give clients advice about divorcing or not, but the myth that loving another is based upon a feeling that may or may not be there and is the only decisive reason for divorcing is often quickly reputed. Feelings come and go, it's the choice that remains. This is a relief for many people to hear.

This is why it is wise for singles to think over if marriage is really what they want. It's a serious choice, a choice that you have to give quite a lot up for to make. In many ways, life as a single can be easier. When making decisions, you only have yourself to consider. Life together is maybe more beautiful and has more depth, but it also asks more from your time, energy, and investment, and marriage will require adjustments (especially if you've lived alone for ten years). You have to adapt to another rhythm, other habits, and other choices that have to do with finances or career. Marrying at thirty is a bit different than marrying at twenty (and right out of your childhood home).

Marriage, as Keller reminds us, is God's gift to us. It's the only place where we can truly experience perfect union with each other on this earth. Does this mean that you as a single are incomplete? Churches can often give that impression, especially if you are attending a wedding service. About this, Keller says, a partner can reprogramme your self image, but marriage is a mirror of the Big Wedding Jesus will one day have with the church. The real saviour is not your husband or your wife, it's Christ. He completes us.

The strength in what Keller writes is his full recognition of the longing to be married. He doesn't say that you shouldn't want to get married. But he says that your focus, your goal is no longer a search for 'the One.' The One is God, and God only. 'The One' doesn't exist outside of God; at most there is that special person, a friend, the friend who you will share the rest of your life with. But this way you'll never miss out on finding 'The One'. If singleness is already a problem, then it is entirely for those who live without God. The search for 'the One' that you see described in many TV programmes or novels is actually a reflection of the search for the God that we're all looking for, whether consciously or unconsciously.

Yet the desire for marriage is more than just a desire for God. In a healthy marriage you see God's love in action. As one of my married girlfriends put it, "Marriage sometimes teaches me about God's grace, when I notice my husband being gracious to me. That he takes me as I am. When he just ignores a stupid mistake I made. It's because we are Christians and believe in God's grace for us, that we can also choose to be kind to each other, accepting each other as we are. For me this is a marriage goal, and it feels then like something's being completed and I realize how much more Jesus 'tolerates' me. What real love is."

If you've been raised as a Christian then you know that ultimately you are searching for God. But if I look around me at a neighbourhood full of single yuppies, I know that they don't know that it is God they're looking for. That the fulfilment, the ultimate unity that they crave can only be found in God. So they keep searching. In bars, on websites, on speed dates. They look and look and don't find it. They jump from one relationship to the other until they feel empty. They won't readily admit it until their thirties, but at a certain age you hear it more and more often:

"Ultimately I'm just looking for somebody to share the rest of my life with." That's why the myth of 'the One' has such power. We all want so badly to feel loved, to be the only 'One' for someone else. We all long for unconditional love.

Connectedness

Okay. Beautiful, this complete-in-God story. One might think that it should be fully embraced by singles in the church. But this isn't true, and if it was, what would I do about it? *I just want to be in a relationship*, would be my answer to the question. Yes, of course it's true that you're complete if God is in your life. But God cannot hold me when I'm sad. God doesn't have arms, at least, not arms I can feel, physically. God does not give wrapped gifts, and he does not make chicken soup when I am sick. What do I need God for then? In the course we give a basic model (see image) for the connectedness we experience with God, ourselves, our friends and the people we date[10].

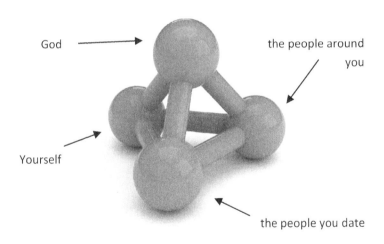

God ⟶   the people around you

Yourself

the people you date

Image: being connect to God, yourself, the people around you and the people you date, is the foundation of Dare to Date.

One is never separate from the other. We give weekly dating assignments. The first date is with God, the second is with yourself, the third with your (married) friend, and at last the fourth date is someone from the opposite gender.

Dating God may sound rather abstract. But for me personally, as well as for many others who have followed this course, these have been the best dates. God doesn't want us to keep our longings and desires to ourselves, he wants to hear about them. He knows all about them, but still he wants us to tell him. "Hello, here I am, and the fact that I'm alone is *painful*. It's not only the being alone, but the rejections I get from time to time. With each rejection I think, *Is it ever going to happen? How much longer?* That is exactly what we can tell God on the first date. Naked and vulnerable. We can tell him about all of our real feelings, longings, doubts, and accusations. What a relief. There is no need to pretend in the presence of God.

It is fascinating how the Bible makes almost no distinction between the longing a man has for a woman (and the other way around), and the longing the people of God have for Christ's return. Although that desire first was a curse, given to the woman in Genesis at the occurrence of the Fall, in the New Testament it is also a holy, God-given desire. It is a healthy, normal, and human longing. Each person is a social creature, made for connection, made for togetherness. The church will bloom when Jesus arrives. In the same way a human being will bloom when he or she has a helper. This desire is known to God. We don't have to, but we're invited to bring this desire to him and ask him for a partner.

In its extreme form, desire can become coveting, and according to Genesis this is part of the curse. "And your desire will be for your husband," and "He will rule over you." This can explain why women generally seem to suffer more from their singleness than men. Men feel similar about their singleness, but are better at

72

distracting themselves, burying themselves in work, sports, and friends. They think less about their singleness if distracted by something else.

Part of this has to do with the differences in male and female brains. A male brain is organized in such a way that the man can always be task-oriented. A woman's brain is wired more relationship-oriented. This difference in orientation creates a difference in focus. A man focusing on his task is completely focused. For a woman, the people involved in the task are the most important. This doesn't mean that men don't desire relationships. So many men have told me how much they long for a relationship and family, and how difficult it is not to know when it will happen.

Desperate Women

Even though men as well as women are longing for a relationship, the worst thing you can appear to be as a single woman is be "desperate." Or at least look desperate. Yet many women feel more desperate than many men for good reason: the ticking biological clock. This is a growing feeling of, "If I want children then I better hurry up," which can slowly begin to dominate a woman's life. A friend of mine, who recently gave birth, was in a pregnancy class with nine women around forty years old. Another friend, who became a mother at twenty-four, was interviewed by a university newspaper for being a "young mother."

According to the medical community, we are waiting too long to have children, and unfortunately there is a deadline around the age of forty that is quickly approaching some of the single women I know. In fact, from the age of thirty, women can already begin their forties approaching and acknowledge their need to 'pick up the pace.' As if that's not enough, the medical professionals have also decided to treat us as urgent cases. Giving birth too late is unhealthy for both mother and child. The risks are greater, the body is less adaptable, and the child has more chances of having an abnormality.

Despite the risks, we do have options. If we decide we want children at a certain age, it's often possible. If it doesn't come naturally, then you can take matters into your own hands, by freezing your eggs for example. You can still become pregnant when it works for you. This is how it worked for a woman in Switzerland who gave birth at the age of sixty-six.

In the preface of his book *Captivating* John Eldredge wrote, ''The mystery of the feminine heart was meant to be a good thing, by the way. A source of joy. Yet it has become a source of shame – women almost universally feel that they are "too much" and "not what they should be". And men tend to pull away from the deeper waters of a woman's soul, unsure of what they will find there or how to handle it.'[11]

This describes exactly how it feels in the course. All of the men's issues about singleness and dating are readily discussable. Most men admit that they needed a kick in the rear or an encouraging push forward, that they benefited by learning about their insecurities. But for the women...it is the recognition of their desire that is so powerful. They can get past their anger, their tough attitudes to men (all men are losers), past their pain, their vulnerability. And from there they often soften, becoming more beautiful and more accessible.

We always have one session in the course where we put men and women into two groups. A woman who was single for a long time before she married speaks to the women, the same with the men.

The men always come back from their session enthusiastic and full of energy, ready and willing to get back on the search. They literally stand outside the door where the women meet, cheering. We send them away, because at the women's session the atmosphere is almost always different. The women are breaking down.

This may be because they've always been strong and kept it together, or blamed men for the fact that they still aren't in a relationship. It's not our goal for people to break down in tears, but it happens often and is often necessary. It's in this time that many of the women make an important switch: they're finally seeing, recognizing, and feeling the pain of being alone.

And this is allowed, even welcomed as an important part of the process. Often women have the tendency to hide or downplay their desire to be married or have children out of a fear of appearing desperate. But because of this, they often don't often feel good in their own skin. Like a thirty-nine year old woman told me in an interview, "Now that I'm in a relationship and am pregnant, I recognise how strong my desire for a child has been, and that it was always there and stronger than I wanted to admit. I now want to go back in time and tell myself it's ok. It's ok to miss that, it's ok to long for a family, and it's ok to admit that it hurts not having that yet."

Holy Longing

Recognising these feelings is important and necessary. Singles can learn to distinguish their healthy desire for a relationship from an unhealthy way of dealing with that desire. The desire for a relationship is a good desire. Being controlled by this desire or being obsessed with having it met is unhealthy. The happy single is a myth, it is actually someone who has buried his or her longings deep inside.

Nobody talks about happily married people. Why is this? Because everyone understands that as a married person you have good days and bad days, alone and together. It's the same with being single. You have your ups and your downs. The only thing is, denying your desire for a relationship in an attempt to not appear desperate is not so good. And then you go around trying to prove that you're really a 'happy single.' Who are you trying to convince?

The longing for a relationship (and children) may find its rightful place in your life. This means it's no longer the overpowering feeling of, "I'm not complete yet" or "If I could just be in a relationship, then..." What it's about is recognising that you have the desire, instead of it having you. If you recognise that being single or married is not "day and night," but rather a difference between a spring sun and a summer sun. Then singleness doesn't only mean a place of pain, sadness, and fear ("Will I ever?") but a place of possibilities. Because, as a friend once said, "The summer sun is nice and hot, but the spring sun makes everything bloom."

If you're able to take an honest look at your singleness, in all its longings and sadness, then and only then can you open your heart to new possibilities. If you acknowledge the feelings are there, then you can learn how to deal with them, and this makes you more inviting to the possibility of a new relationship. When you recognise your longings in a healthy way, then that longing becomes a holy longing.[12] A longing for the wholeness that God has intended for his creation. A longing for unity. A longing arisen from the fact that God created man and woman and saw that it was 'good' that the two become one.

In this chapter I have highlighted a few problems singles face. In the rest of this book we're always going to take a look at possible solutions for these problems. But before that I want to make it clear that singleness in and of itself is not a problem. In fact, it's not for nothing that in 1 Corinthians 7 Paul argues that it's better to remain unmarried in certain circumstances. He says this within a certain context to a specific group, which we'll talk about more in the next chapter.

Questions to discuss

1. What are the statistics like where you live? Single vs married, in church and outside?
2. Do you believe it's better to be married?
3. Is loneliness an issue for you?
4. To what extent do you do embrace your singleness?
5. What about dating?
6. How do you like the idea of 'Becoming the One' rather than looking for 'the One'?
7. If you could ask Jesus one question regarding your singleness, what would it be?
8. How would it be for you to date from connectedness? Would it change the experience?

Part 2

The Bible and Dating

Chapter 3
The Old Testament and Dating

Then the Lord God said, "It is not good that the man should be alone; I will make him a helper fit for him" (...) and brought her to the man. Then the man said, "This at last is bone of my bones and flesh of my flesh; she shall be called Woman, because she was taken out of Man."

Genesis 2:18-23 (NBV)

Introduction

In part two I want to dive into the passages in the Bible about dating and going about relationships. I'm often asked in workshops and seminars what the Bible says about dating. Despite the fact that the Bible doesn't give many direct teachings about this subject, there are many valuable lessons to be learned from its various stories. Keep in mind that I am reading these stories from a certain perspective. Of course there are other layers of meaning to be found within these stories which are also important. But it's good to note that these are my own interpretations of these stories, applied to the topic we're now discussing: singleness.

The First Match in the Bible

Eve was given to Adam before the Fall, and thus marriage was created in Eden, well before anything went wrong. Marriage is not everything, but was essentially intended as the crown of creation. Creation was not complete with the creation of man. God said that it "wasn't good" when he saw that Adam was alone.

I've always been intrigued by how Adam and Eve "found" each other. I've often asked myself why God didn't create Eve at the same time as Adam. In Genesis 1 the Lord God speaks in general of creating man(kind), creating them "male and female." It also says at the end of the chapter that God looked at everything he had made and saw that it was "very good" (Genesis 1:31). But the story that follows describes humankind's very first love story. God saw Adam, and Adam was already good: complete, finished. But, also alone in the sense of 'on his own.' After God created Adam, he said, "It is good." What is striking here is that he also says this at the end of each day of creation. Apparently he sees that Adam's aloneness "is not good." (Genesis 2:18).

Adam is first put to work. This is his first task, working. He is to give all the animals a name, which would have been quite a task. Perhaps he wasn't quite ready and needed some time before Eve came into his life.

Did God somehow want Adam to feel what it meant to be alone? Adam lacked nothing; he had food and drink, a nice job, a place to sleep and the companionship of the almighty God. And still he finds himself alone. Within the animals there are masculine and feminine versions within the same species. They complement each other, can reproduce. But why does God notice only *after* he creates Adam that it is "not good for man to be alone"? Couldn't God have anticipated this? It seems almost cruel that God created the animals to be in pairs, but that he set man alone in the world and immediately gave him such a big task.

Does Adam complain about his alone-ness? We don't read about this in the text. He doesn't say to God, "I don't get why you're not giving me a partner." But still Adam appears to be missing something, because the text goes onto say, "but for Adam there was not a helper fit for him" (Genesis 2:20). He sees all the animals but misses his own kind. And apparently he's in search for something, otherwise it wouldn't be noted. How much time did he have to think about this? Most single men that I know appear not to dwell on it. It's only when you ask them, that they admit that they would like a girlfriend. This is why I think that Adam also had this feeling of being alone. This seems evidenced in his overjoyed reaction when he cries out something like, "Finally, someone like me!"

God puts Adam in a deep sleep. Typical! The first relationship begins with a sleeping man. We're getting sidetracked for a moment, but how many sleeping men can we count in the average church? According to the writers David Murrow, author of the book *Why Men Hate Going to Church,* and Larry Crabb, author of *The Silence of Adam,* there are quite a few. Many men have the tendency to be a bit bashful when it comes what actions they should take when it comes to beginning a relationship. They're also called, "silent men." Passive. Many of the women I talk to become angry when they mention this, they see it as apathy. It causes real disappointment and actually also sadness. As women they feel unseen. Then it's the men's turn to feel angry. They're doing their best but their actions are often rejected. "It's never good enough," a friend once told me. "Whatever I do. First I'm too nice, and then I'm too blunt. I have to be patient and wait, but then I'm supposed to do the right thing at the right time. I just don't know anymore."

While Adam slept, God took one of his ribs. God built the woman from strong material, a part of Adam himself. Flesh of his flesh, bone of his bone. There was a physical connection before there was a spiritual or emotional connection. And God himself brought the woman to Adam, on his arm, into the garden toward her future spouse.

There are so many women who break away from the arm of their father and race into the garden. *Not me, I'm not sitting around waiting. I'm going to find him. And when I find him, I'm going to drag him by the hair into my life*, they seem to think. The result is that they seem surprised when the aforementioned man gets "cold feet," or that he doesn't seem engaged any more, or that he turns and runs as soon as he sees a woman coming after him. They are hurt, and then place the blame on the entire male population. "Men disgust me. They're wimps, wusses, so passive." And the louder these women cry this, the more often the men in question withdraw. Not very helpful, this vicious cycle.

When God brings Eve to him, Adam is just opening his eyes. Something amazing happens when he sees her for the first time. Adam joyfully and loudly exclaims, "Finally! There she is! She is like me, and she is mine." Was she the one for Adam? She seems to have been. But he had no choice; neither of them had a choice. We will never know Eve's version of the story. You are made and immediately brought to a man. You barely have the time to realize that you're alive, and boom, you're married. For the single woman, this story doesn't really illuminate how to behave before you are brought to your husband. As a man, you can at least get started with work until your wait is over. But as a woman? The beautiful thing is that after this, they begin their work together. That is their mission: working together as equal partners.

In the 90s, a fragment of American evangelicals developed a whole movement focused on courtship. According to this movement, as a single woman you can best live with your parents until they decide whether or not you should be dating someone. A man may ask for your hand in marriage only if he has asked your father's permission. This is supposed to be based upon the biblical principles, if you dig through all the way back to the image given in Genesis 2 of God giving the woman to Adam. With Joshua Harris's book *I Kissed Dating Goodbye* this movement received a great following. Thankfully Harris finally this year (2019) decided to withdraw his book from the shelves. Unfortunately he does this decades too late and the damage is done for many singles. They decide praying and waiting is the safest option to find a partner. Except, they don't find anyone and no one finds them.

An important question to ask yourself is what kind of God do you imagine God to be? What does it mean to you that God is like a father and you are like a child? Are you really still a small child? Does your father have to make all your choices for you, maybe literally, with the man who will come into your life? Or are you his child, but also one who lives an adult and independent life, part of which is looking for a partner to share life with?

The Fall and How Everything Changed

And then– the Fall. The woman who was given to the man played a very crucial role. She experimented with her freedom of choice. And what did Adam do? He was silent. In *The Silence of Adam* Larry Crabb talks about this. The silence of some Christian men can be deafening. They feel incompetent in the church. Churches are more focused on women's issues, on loving each other, on "warm and inviting." Not on challenge, adventure, or heroism. The skills that you need in a church are social, you have to be willing to sing, and above all else, surrender. These are not skills that men easily feel competent in. And if men don't feel competent, most would prefer to stay away rather than fail. Society gives men the message that they have to do it right and well, that it's important to control the situation and think of solutions. He's practiced in this. But the church asks something very different from its members, especially its men.

Is it the men who must change? I think that women, married or unmarried, could do a bit more to learn about and understand men.[13] This could benefit the atmosphere in both marriages and the church. It's also good for men to know more about women. (Hint: we're different, but maybe not that much. We all want to be respected and loved, men and women alike.)

For many women, it is in their nature to love. Yet it appears that many women within the church are holding back their love until they have a man to direct it toward. That's too bad, because their love is badly needed in so many places. Look for example, at the children within the church. How many of them come from broken families? A loving adoptive aunt is not only helpful, but for many children the difference between having a safe adult in their life or not. To be a mentor, a friend, a spiritual mum to someone, someone who eases the loneliness of another being, is the most important thing in life.

As a woman you are called to be many things besides a wife and mother. You're also a sister, friend, daughter, aunt, coach, or mentor. As a man you're called to be many things besides a husband and father. You're a brother, friend, son, uncle, coach, or mentor. If you're bypassing these rolls in search of 'the one,' you're missing out on a lot. And the experience of what else you're called to be can sometimes soften the longing or pain that you feel for the roles you're still missing.

It's in men's nature to respect. Men often find it easier to respect a woman than to love her.[14] Sadly, so many men in the church continue to be respectful while forgetting to decidedly act upon their own course of action. Even before the Fall, God asks men to take the lead in relationships, to leave their parents and to search for a wife. As Genesis 2:24 reads, "Therefore a man shall leave his father and mother and cling fast to his wife, and they shall become one flesh."

We also often read that God has created man to be the "head of the family." Many a woman shudders at this text, as if she is meant to be subservient, inferior. But isn't it actually a beautiful interaction? Personally I'm convinced that a man will flourish if he feels seen and respected as a man. And yes, the woman might also want to be appreciated. I do know a lot of women who say, "I don't want him to admire me from afar, I want him to know and understand me." She wants someone to love her.

A colleague of mine, also a therapist, views the male/female difference in a positive light. She says, "If men and women were too much like each other and could fulfill the other's every need, we wouldn't need God anymore." This is why a good marriage has the "triple cord." God must have a place in our marriages, just as he did in our single lives. We would not notice our need for him if we all had perfect marriages. Male and female differences may therefore be necessary to maintain our need for and connection with God. At the same time, it is precisely these differences that can lead to the biggest friction and hurt.

After the Fall, there is a curse. The "woman's desire will be for her husband," but the husband will often be unavailable, working hard for his bread. "He shall rule over her," the text reads. Today, the meaning of 'rule over' may be more emotional than physical. The man dominates through his absence, his emotional unavailability. At the end of their lives, many men express regret with how much time they spent working, realizing that it has been at the cost of their relationship with their family.

Cloud regularly refers to "relational strength." Relational strength is the ability to enter into a relationship, to connect with someone else. If a man works too hard, he sometimes does not use his emotional strength enough. Not because it's not there, but because his focus is elsewhere. Often women are blamed for wanting men who are taller than they are, bigger or stronger, or a man who has an expensive car or a high salary. A strong build and a good salary are both symbols of power. What women are interested in lies behind the symbols: the ability to stand up for you, to fight for you if necessary. When men show this, women are impressed[15].

The Well

The Old Testament is full of laws and regulations, but none of them are about relationships. This is particularly evident in books about sexuality and what is permissible sexual behavior for marriage, or topics like masturbation. The point is this: the Bible doesn't have specific information related to these topics. The only guideline you can be sure of is the following: don't make too many hard and fast statements about what the Bible says. What we're discussing is a topic that is culturally determined, and did not exist in biblical times as it does today.

People in Old Testament Israel were married young. The women were still girls, many as young as fourteen when they were married, with men a bit older. Men were considered to be full adults around the age of thirty. This age difference would be difficult to swallow today, but in that time it was very normal. It was also normal for a man to have multiple wives, or even slaves as concubines. That speaks volumes for the idea of specific laws: there is no gold standard. Establishing relationships is as human as eating and drinking, working or sleeping, and the interpretation of the specifics is determined by the time and culture you live in, and not by a set of rules from those above you.

What, then, can you know? Actually it's very simple. In Genesis 24 Abraham is looking for a wife for his son. Isaac appears not to have to do the looking himself, and it probably also wasn't a simple task because he lived in a land full of Canaanites, among women Abraham didn't want for his son. Nor was Isaac allowed to leave, because Abraham had promised God that he and his descendants would stay in the land where they were living, land God would give them. So the woman had to be found elsewhere.

The mission that Abraham's servant was given is intriguing: go to a place where you can find suitable candidates, women with the same origins and beliefs. The servant not only finds such a land, but he chooses a strategic spot within that land: the well. The well is a reoccurring backdrop for the romances in the Bible. Not only does Abraham's servant find a wife for Isaac, but we read in Genesis 29 that Jacob first meets his beloved wife, Rachel, at a well. Later we read in Exodus 2 how Moses first encounters his wife Zipporah, you guessed it, at a well.

In that time the well was a place of meeting. Everyone had to make a daily visit to draw water, but it was a social place where news and gossip was exchanged, a place to be together. It was a gathering place for the community, just as a church building is today for Christians, and a bar can be for many others. It was actually quite bold for these men to pay a visit when they knew the women would be there. It was customary for men and women to visit the well at different times of the day.

Let's go back to Abraham's servant, the first matchmaker mentioned after God himself in Genesis 2. In Genesis 24:7 Abraham advises his servant to allow God's leading. "He will send his angel before you, and you shall take a wife for my son from there." The 'how' is not completely clear. In verse 21 it appears that the servant also doesn't know how this is to be done. Earlier in the story he had a very specific prayer that God would give him a sign that the right woman would not only give him water but his animals as well. This is quite a tall order, because drawing water from the well was a difficult chore. And for a woman encountering a strange man, this was quite something to ask. But the servant got his sign, exactly as he'd asked, yet he still doesn't appear entirely convinced. Verse 21 reads, "The man gazed at her in silence to learn if he'd prospered of his journey or not." Hello, even after receiving the exact sign he'd asked for! But apparently a period of doubt seems to be part of the dating process.

In the end it's the servant who has to fish or cut bait, not the angel he had hoped to lead him or even God himself through many signs and wonders. The servant has to decide whether or not to speak his intentions to the girl. It's not only up to the man to decide. In verse 8 Abraham states emphatically, "But if the woman is not willing to follow you, then you will be free from this oath of mine; only you must not take my son back there." The woman, we learn, has the freedom to choose. She does not have to choose for this new life. She may say 'no.' Her opinion also matters, and she too has responsibility for the choice she makes.

The servant has said his piece. He offers her gifts and asks if he may stay with her father. When she assents, actually tells him that there's more than enough room, the servant falls on his face thanking God. Beautiful. He's made his decision, but is aware of the relationship between his own responsibility and God's lead. The girl's answer, a warm, generous welcome, is confirmation of all he had hoped and prayed for.

The point seems to be: it is always both/and. Yes, God *both* leads *and* the decision is yours. This tension between one's own responsibility and God's sovereignty and guidance is explored by diverse theologians. I don't know if we'll ever be completely sure about where God's sovereignty ends and our responsibility begins. I do know that the Bible is full of stories of people who must make the right choices, and pursuing what is good and right. Just as it is written in Philippians 4:6-8: "...Do not be anxious about anything, but in everything by prayer and supplication with thanksgiving let your requests be made known to God. And the peace of God, which surpasses all understanding, will guard your hearts and your minds in Christ Jesus. Finally, brothers, whatever is true, whatever is honorable, whatever is just, whatever is pure, whatever is lovely, whatever is commendable, if there is any excellence, if there is anything worthy of praise, think about these things."

You Always Marry the Wrong Person

It turns out that the girl at the well was named Rebekah. The funny thing is that she leaves the servant standing there, waiting for more clarity, just as much later her niece Rachel would cause her son Jacob to wait, and just as Zipporah and her sisters leave Moses waiting. The gentlemen have much more work to do to fully win the hearts of the ladies. And once hearts are won, it is really just the beginning... Theologian Stanley Hauerwas, once formulated 'the law of Hauerwas.' According to this law, you never marry the right person, but you learn how to be married to the wrong person and become the right person for them.

Now Rebekah's brother Laban comes into the scene. Advocates of courtship may ask themselves uneasily where the father was, but he probably had other things on his mind. Or maybe he had sent his son to deal with it. It seems as though Laban likes to involve himself in matters of the heart, as is evident when his nephew Jacob returns later in search of a wife. Laban goes to the servant, most likely because he saw the jewellery the servant had given to his sister. Does he smell money? We don't know. At that time a woman to be married would bring in something financially to the family.

Any way, we see that Laban is kindness itself. "Come in, O blessed of the LORD" (Genesis 24:31). The servant tells the whole story from A to Z, and Rebekah's father Bethuel, who has joined the party, seems to conclude that this is the right way to proceed. 'This thing has come from the LORD...the LORD has spoken" (verse 50). This is a beautiful interaction between leadership and responsibility, because the servant's story is full of the measures not only that he has taken, but also Rebekah and Laban's efforts until they find themselves in the discussion they're in. Just like the man working his acreage: praying alone for God's blessing won't get you far, but it is prayer and effort working together that has the greatest effect.

They spend their night there. The next day Rebekah's brother and mother say, "Of course she can go with you, but give her another week or so." Only after they speak is Rebekah consulted. They have probably already decided that it's a very good idea for her to go with this servant to be with the rich man who lives very far away. In that time marriage was not about love, and definitely not about romance, or the notion of "love at first sight." Rebekah would never say that the 'spark' wasn't there; she hadn't even met her groom yet! Marriage was primarily a business transaction. Not marrying meant that you would not have children. You lived on through your children. Without children the thought was that nothing of you would be carried on. Therefore not marrying and having children wasn't an option. So Rebekah left with the servant.

Now the fairytale can begin. They seem to know one another from afar, it seems. He comes to meet her and she sees him approaching. Unfortunately the writer apparently had no feel for drama, otherwise he would elaborated on this part of the story. In verse 67 he limits himself to, "and she became his wife, and he loved her." Still, this one sentence reveals a lot of information. He took her as his wife, that was first. And then, later, he loved her.

Walter Trobisch wrote about this in the book *I loved a Girl*. An old Indian proverb says, "Marrying is like putting a cold pan on a warm fire and then waiting for the contents to slowly warm up. You (in the western world) put a hot pan on a warm fire and then wait until the contents of the pan slowly become cold'. What this proverb is saying is that we here in the West often begin our relationships with fiery passion and intense infatuation, but invest far too little in the growth of real love, while the other way around, those who are married before the love is there, can grow to love. Many arranged marriages become, after a time, close, loving marriages. This is probably also how it worked in biblical times.

Jacob in Love

The next story at the well goes differently. Jacob sees Rachel and is instantly and madly in love. The story is quite dramatic. "As soon as Jacob saw Rachel (...) he came near and rolled the stone from the well's mouth and watered the flock of his mother's brother. Then Jacob kissed Rachel and wept aloud." (Genesis 29:10-11). This is Hollywood. Swelling violin music, singing birds, a cloudless sky, true love in action. Right? Or could it be (sorry to spoil the moment) pure lust? Laban, who has learned what a situation like this can mean, sees dollar signs. It could be that from past experience he knows that a man in love will do whatever it takes to win his prize.

Laban takes advantage of the situation. "Tell me what you will give for her. Name your price." "Seven years of work!" cries Jacob in his amour. Apparently Jacob didn't have silver or gold to offer. Laban (of course) agrees with the offer. Jacob gets to work, and the text tells us, "they seemed to him but a few days because of the love he had for her." All of this time they had remained unmarried. Would they have slept together? That doesn't seem to fit the times, but being in love for seven years without any physical encouragement also seems unlikely. Regardless, this can happen in Hollywood and it is incredibly romantic.

Either way, after seven years Jacob did marry one of Laban's daughters, but it was Leah instead of Rachel. Laban had probably hoped that in the seven years that had passed, a man would come along for Leah, so that he could marry her off first. At least that was the intention, the older daughter marrying before the younger. Apparently men were not in great abundance. Was this because Leah was unattractive? Nowhere in the Bible do you read as clearly as you do in this story that someone is ugly. And this isn't because of all of her outer qualities, but her eyes are specifically mentioned: they didn't shine. Why didn't her eyes shine? In my practice I regularly see depressive people, or people who are suffering from burnout. They often have eyes that don't shine. Shine is a sign of happiness, of zest for life. For Leah, it's probably less about physical attractiveness than it is about a lack of joy, which makes her unattractive.

Sometimes I imagine how this would have been for Leah. Such a fun, attractive sister, the kind of girl a guy is so in love with he'll work for your father seven years to win her. And then your father tells you that you must marry this man. You know what's coming: at a certain moment after you are left alone in your sleeping quarters he's going to wake up and realize you're Leah, and not Rachel, the one he is so in love with. How awful. But maybe part of her is happy, knowing that now at least she can have children. Maybe I'm making her position sadder than it needs to be with my western, 21st century perspective.

Veiled during the ceremony, Leah is married off to Jacob. After the wedding Jacob is in a state when he discovers he has married 'the wrong' sister. Too bad that Jacob hadn't read Hauerwas ("You always marry the wrong person"). He demands to have Rachel. Laban seems to understand this, and still he takes his chance. Jacob may marry Rachel immediately, if he keeps working for Laban for seven more years.

Jacob keeps his preference. None too subtly, the text tells us that "Jacob loved Rachel more than Leah." In short, Jacob is and remains in love. The story is nearly bursting with these emotions. Still, nothing goes as planned. Even after Jacob marries the love of his life, there are more than enough disappointments. Rachel is unable to get pregnant. The story doesn't end with "they lived happily ever after," a reminder that real life is no fairytale.

The Old Testament is saturated with dramatic love stories. In many of these stories, however, the drama tends toward the dysfunctional. Jacob's daughter, Dinah, sleeps with a guy named Sichem, an outsider. Dinah's brothers take revenge by murdering Sichem's entire family. Onan fails to get his widowed sister-in-law pregnant, although that's his responsibility to his brother. Joseph escapes the seduction of Potiphar's wife, David lusts after Bathsheba, another man's wife, and so it goes. There are good times and bad times. The theme is not often love and fidelity. Strangely enough, the Bible shows many examples of sex and lust, seduction and revenge, about egocentrism.

The Church as a Modern Well

Back to the well. Further on in Exodus chapter 2, we'll find Moses there. He has fled, far from his home and family. He ends up in Midian, and goes directly to the well there to sit and wait. I often notice how effectively the church can act as a well, as a place of community. Wherever you may find yourself in the world, there is a big chance that you'll find a warm welcome inside the doors of a church. A home away from home.

At least I believe this is the way church was meant to be. Even though the church is one of the most vulnerable places I know, susceptible to gossip, disputes, and troubles, it is also one of the most powerful places. A well that will never run dry. So Moses finds the well in Midian, sits, and waits. It's still not clear what for.

Soon we see objects in the distance making their way toward the well – seven beautiful young ladies. He jumps up in a hurry to help them by fending off shepherds in order to water their herd.

Another father makes his way into the scene. When the sisters arrive home, their father, Reuel, asks them why they were back so soon. "An Egyptian delivered us out of the hand of the shepherds"...He said to his daughters, "Then where is he? Why have you left the man? Call him, that he may eat bread" (Exodus 2:20). Moses arrives and stays as a guest until Reuel gives him his daughter Zipporah to marry. Zipporah obeys her father and marries Moses. And although the rest of the story never reveals if their marriage ever became "true love," it does appear evident that Moses has a brave wife who returns with him to Egypt. She even circumcises her own son when her husband fails to (Exodus 4:25). A good match doesn't always mean love alone.

Daring Ruth (and Naomi too)

After reading much further, we come to Ruth. In between are all kinds of more or less spectacular stories about successful or failed relationships. Take Samson, for example, the guy who just had to marry a Philistine woman "for he was seeking an opportunity against the Philistines" (Judges 14:4). Apparently from time to time God saw marriage as purely strategic. Ruth's second marriage also had more of a social than a romantic purpose, it was primarily about redemption. Even so, we will look mostly at the romantic aspects of this story.

After the death of her husband and father-in-law, Ruth decides to stay by her mother-in-law's side. They move to Naomi's homeland, a land that is completely foreign to Ruth, to live among people that aren't her people. So we know already that Ruth is daring, but we don't know just how daring quite yet. Whose idea it was isn't entirely clear, but in Ruth 2 we read a very subtle text that begins, "Now Naomi had a relative of her husband's, a worthy man of the clan of Elimelech, whose name was Boaz."

These could be the first words of a movie trailer. "It went something like this..." He was family. Ruth and Naomi arrived in the new land at the beginning of the barley harvest, and Ruth wanted to glean the fields, which means picking up the leftovers after the harvesters had been through. Verse 3 reads, "So she set out and went and gleaned in the field after the reapers, and she happened to come to the part of the field belonging to Boaz, who was of the clan of Elimelech." A man of whom we were already aware, so rich and important and available as he was. Notice how verse three begins with *she happened to* and not *God led her to.*

Boaz keeps an eye on Ruth, as the story goes. He notices her, the immigrant, and refers to her as "my daughter," and gives her privileges. He tells his workers to leave extras from the harvest for her to glean. When Ruth asks him why he's doing this, he replies, full of admiration for her and what she's done in staying by her mother-in-law's side. Boaz does much to express his care for her. This rich, important guy has the heart and eyes to see how people on his land live. Or maybe he is in love. Or both. We're not told. But he is clearly not brave enough to take further steps with Ruth.

Naomi is brave enough. She hears the story from Ruth, laughs, and says, "Come on, we're going to work on that guy." It takes a while, one harvest follows another, but still Boaz hasn't come further in pursuing Ruth. So Naomi says, "Put on your prettiest dress and make sure you smell nice, because if he's not coming to you, you must go to him. Go lay at his feet." How would that be for you, gentlemen, after a good party to find that a woman had crawled into bed with you and lay down at your feet? In her prettiest dress and sprayed with her sweetest perfume? This would make things considerably easier.

Keep in mind that Ruth doesn't seduce Boaz sexually, and she also doesn't propose to him. "Come on, Boaz, let's get married already." What she says is much subtler. Actually what she says is, "If you ask me to marry you, I will say yes. Not out of lust or even love, but because of a need for protection and security." How many ladies can relate to this? Today women have the tendency to take the lead, whether single or married, because they think, "If I don't do something, nothing will happen."

A friend of mine always emphasizes how men should be invited to take the lead. He says, "If women can learn how to be inviting to a man that they like without pushing him, then they're helping that man take more action and show initiative." According to him, many men go quickly for the "easily available" women, while passing over the intelligent women with the more complex personality out of fear of being rejected. What these women could definitely do more is to be inviting to a man and let him know of her interest, without making the first move. It appears to be all about subtlety.

Luckily, Ruth had a mother-in-law that gave her advice and suggestions. The involvement of your community can play an important role in relational formation. Boaz, as it turns out, has certainly thought of possibilities, primarily about the role he can play as kinsman-redeemer. When the moment becomes clear to him that he sees Ruth as the one he wants to be with, he says, "I know that you're worth the effort. You're special; you could have chosen for a younger or richer man, but you came here." And the rest is history.

Jeremiah, Alone and Unhappy

From all the singles that we know of in the Bible, there are only a few who received a explicit calling to singleness. This is the case with Jeremiah, and meant for his whole life. Many singles in the Bible are single only for a certain period of time. Take Moses, who was without a wife until his forties, or Mary, Martha, and Lazarus, siblings whose spouses aren't mentioned and so we can assume didn't yet exist. It doesn't mean that they were definitely single, it is possible that their spouses simply didn't play a role in the story. Either way, it wasn't important to the biblical authors to mention the detail of their relational status.

I'm sometimes disturbed by the way speakers are introduced at Christian conferences. If they're married, this must be explicitly stated, along with the number of children. If no spouse or children is mentioned, then you can be sure the speaker is single. Why is this? And why doesn't anybody introduce a speaker as single? I think it has to do with the perceived added value of being married. Don't we place too big an emphasis on this in the Christian world? What does being married or single have to do with your personality or skills? Does being married give credibility to the speaker?

Jeremiah receives a clear calling to remain single for his entire life. In Jeremiah 16 the text tells us that God tells him that, "you shall not take a wife, neither shall you have sons and daughters in this place." This is so shockingly unheard of in this time, that the Old Testament doesn't even have a word for 'bachelor.' Not having children is the most shocking. Procreation was seen as an essential part of creating the family line that would lead to the arrival of the Messiah. Not having children was unthinkable, it meant a definitive and final death for you as a family.

What follows is a very unhappy Jeremiah who does nothing but complain to God. He's not called the "crying prophet" for nothing. English even has the noun 'jeremiad' meaning a complaining tirade. But Jeremiah does have reason to complain. He has to constantly bring the most upsetting messages to Israel with all kinds of allusions to being unfaithful and other nasty comparisons. This wouldn't have made him the most beloved prophet ever. In addition he had to frequently travel, and was prohibited by God from going to parties or funerals. This combination would have ensured a continuous social isolation. And when singleness seems unbearable, it is important for other social contacts to fill the need of closeness and intimacy in other relationships.

His singleness, however, did have a clear goal. God needed Jeremiah to give a message to his people. God had conceived of Jeremiah's calling even before his birth, as we read in Jeremiah 1:5. It was all about consistency: Jeremiah could not do what he did, or said what he said, without living in total loneliness and sobriety. His message wouldn't have had the persuasive power it had if he had been radiantly happy. It's both disconcerting and reassuring to me that God had planned this from before Jeremiah's birth. It's worrisome that God's plan for us may include a shorter or longer time of loneliness in order to accomplish a certain purpose. It's reassuring that God seems to care for us so much that he is involved in the course of our lives.

In my opinion, most of the people who have written the most meaningful things about the subject of singles have been single for longer periods of time, which makes me take them more seriously. I know that it works this way also for our course, that speaking as a single to singles for many people makes me feel trustworthy. I "know" what I'm talking about. At the same time, it is frustrating for some people that although I know exactly "what to do," it apparently hasn't "worked" for me yet. I understand this can be troubling, but I think it says more about them than about the course. The goal of our seminars and workshops is not to get people married. Our goal is to come alongside you whether if you've been single for a long or a short time, and to make the best of it. Just as you, I think, must do as you walk through every God-given phase of your life, as complicated as it sometimes can be. Getting into a relationship is not some trick you can pull off or fail at, making it work out or not.

The beautiful thing is that God provides, even for Jeremiah. He knows what we need, and when we need it. C.S. Lewis says, 'God is both further from us and closer to us than we know. He is the maker, we are his creatures, he is the source, we are flowing from him. For the same reason the intimacy between God and even the lowliest of creatures is closer than the intimacy between creatures'. As is described in Psalm 68, God gives the lonely a home. He promises a place for widows and orphans, and for the childless a multitude of children.

Hosea Marries a Whore

We'd prefer to see God as the author of a perfect romance novel. American Bible teacher and theologian Derek Prince and his second wife Ruth co-authored a book called *God is a Matchmaker*. Prince claims that God told him clearly who he must marry (twice!). Even when he felt no love for said woman, he obeyed and stayed with her until the love was there. Wonderful. But Prince was a busy man, a travelling theologian who had no time to date. Perhaps the message to marry did come from God and he had his own reasons for providing a wife, without having to scroll through a dating website or have coffee with all the single women in his church.

I'm not interested in questioning such experiences. I am interested, however, in explaining that such experiences aren't for everyone, and perhaps this a good thing. In the Bible Hosea is one of the few who is given a specific order to marry a specific woman. Hosea isn't given an exact name, but is allowed to choose within a certain category of women: the prostitutes. Not every man's dream, seems to me. Anyway, Hosea was a prophet, and just as Jeremiah's "not marrying" was to serve an example, so Hosea's marriage to a whore was a metaphor for the people of Israel. It was a way of showing them exactly the kind of behaviour they were displaying. You could say that Hosea's marriage was purely for professional reasons. It allowed the nation of Israel to see something of God's faithfulness to them.

Another plus: Hosea was allowed to choose which unfaithful wife he would marry. God didn't say, "Marry so-and-so." No, he said, "Go, take to yourself a wife of whoredom and have children of whoredom" (Hosea 1:2). Arrange it yourself. And so it was: Hosea married and had children with Gomer. After that, many unkind things were said about Israel, and in passing, also Hosea's wife. But God is still incredibly romantic. "Therefore, behold, I will allure her, and bring her into the wilderness, and speak tenderly to her. And there I will give her vineyards and make the Valley of Achor a door of hope. And there she shall answer as in the days of her youth, as at the time when she came out of the land of Egypt. And in that day, declares the Lord, you will call me 'My Husband,' (Hosea 2:14-16). Hosea's improbable mission appeared probable, after all. Hosea married and even had children, not because his goal was to marry and have children, but because it was to follow God obediently.

God cannot be boxed in, or tamed. God is not a God we can always follow predictably or safely. God is big and compelling, and always very close. Just as we read in Hosea 2:21-22, "And I will betroth you to me forever. I will betroth you to me in righteousness and in justice, in steadfast love and in mercy." Those are the kinds of words that Hollywood could take a lesson from.

God rarely speaks about a calling to be single. If you have this calling, rest assured that you'll be told very clearly. If you, like Hosea, are told very clearly who to marry, then there is a special reason for that. Considering what we've just looked at, there seem to be two basic principles on relational formation in the Old Testament. One, it's not good for a person to be alone (Genesis 2), and two, don't marry an unbeliever (as Abraham did, among others).

It's difficult to get applicable tips from the Bible about dating and relationships in a simple one, two, three. I have still managed to find a few examples in the chapter above. When my course attendees ask, "But dating doesn't exist in the Bible, does it?" then my first reaction is mostly along the lines of, "What about Facebook, iPhones, or apartment buildings? Those aren't in the Bible, either."

Yes, relationship formation is partially culturally determined and limited to a certain period of time. But in the Bible apparently everything has happened in the area of relationship formation, much of what we can learn from, even today. Look at the initiative men are taking to start a relationship, and how they're willing to step out of their comfort zone. Look at the examples of women who have the courage to take a step even when they don't know what the outcome will be, and how they're letting go of control. We can learn a lot from each other!

Questions to discuss

1. How do you feel about reading the Bible searching for stories of dating?

2. Are there stories you'd like to add, Bible passages that have inspired you in your singleness?

3. How do you feel about God creating Eve for Adam? And how about Adam not liking his singleness, complaining to God about it (before sin entered the world!)?

4. What about the well, what's your nearest well? And how easy is it there to interact with single people your age?

5. How do you feel about the concept of always marrying the wrong person?

6. What about working twice seven years for the love of your life, guys, would you be into such an investment?

7. God doesn't seem to address the issue of singleness much, what does that mean to you?

Chapter 4
Dating in the New Testament

Now concerning the betrothed, I have no command from the Lord, but I give my judgment as one who by the Lord's mercy is trustworthy. I think that in view of the present distress it is good for a person to remain as he is. Are you bound to a wife? Do not seek to be free. Are you free from a wife? Do not seek a wife. But if you do marry, you have not sinned, and if a betrothed woman marries, she has not sinned. Yet those who marry will have worldly troubles, and I would spare you that.

1 Corinthians 7:25-28

Introduction

Whereas the Old Testament, beginning in Genesis and continuing in all of the stories about relationships, seems to validate the desire for relationships, the New Testament seems to emphasize the message that only in God are you complete. "You complete me," Tom Cruise tells Renée Zellweger at the end of the film *Jerry Maguire* (yes I am that old). For most women this part is a tear-jerker, but it is also a lie. The only person whom you can say the words "You complete me" to is Jesus. He actually does. As male and female human beings, we will always fail each other and will never perfectly complement another perfectly, let alone complete them. Jesus comes and says come to me, and you'll have enough (Mat 11:28). Paul is trying to emphasize this in his letter to the Corinthians. He's not there to undermine marriage, but he wants to send the clear message that in God's eyes, "even" single, you are complete.

Longing for 'the One'

In the Old Testament, the well was the place to be. In the New Testament, Jesus encounters a woman also at a well (John 4), another raw encounter. Jesus asked her, this woman who has not only a *woman* but a *Samaritan,* of another breed, not Jesus usual in crowd so to say, to draw water for him to drink. He is tired and it is warm, being close to midday. This wasn't really the time to draw water, but this Samaritan woman had a dubious reputation. Others preferred not to be seen with her, and maybe she was also a bit ashamed herself.

So she comes to draw water at the hour that the outcasts come to the well. She comes to the well and finds Jesus there: a Jew, a Rabbi. Jews avoided Samaritans at that point in time, but Jesus stayed where he was. And if that wasn't strange enough, this man asked her for a drink. With the stories of the Old Testament fresh in our minds, we can almost imagine this to be a marriage proposal.

But this woman already has a husband, although at first she denies this. And before this husband she had five others. But this isn't what the conversation is about. Jesus tells her, "You won't find eternal life with these men, and also not eternal happiness. I am your only true love. Only in me are you complete. Come to me and stop searching for your happiness in these men." The world stops.

So much so that the woman, in a very important detail, leaves her jug by the well. For now, she doesn't need the water, even though she came all this way and was so thirsty. She runs to the village where she lives and tells this story. Because of what she says, many come to faith. Quite a powerful witness.

And right there by that well, Jesus smiles. When his disciples return they tell him, "You have to eat something," but Jesus has other priorities. In this case, it's having a healing, therapeutic conversation with an outcast. He opens her eyes more than to what is true, but he also gives her a place within the community. Because of her testimony he is welcome to stay in the village for two more days. There are many people who want to hear his story, who want to follow him. And through the restoration of her place within the community, he's provided a place to find love and healing in the people who surround her. The chance of her throwing herself back into the arms of the next man is considerably less.

Jesus actually says to the woman at the well, "I am your true love." So this is definitely a proposal, but also so much more than that. It is a request to be united forever, in contrast to the marriage vows, "Till death do us part." Jesus calls himself *the one.* He does this in several ways, and the invitation is both romantic and life-saving. *Come to me, I am the way, the truth, and the life. I am the only one who can actually make you whole.* Meeting with God first is essential in finding 'the one.' God is the only real answer to our longings.

A friend once told me how she dreamed that she was terribly thirsty and was trying to drink from a dripping tap. And then someone, she thought might be God, told her, "Look behind you." And there, behind her was an enormous fountain. "That is my love for you," God told her. "If you're looking for love in a man, then you're trying to drink from a dripping faucet." Not that I want to compare men to dripping taps of course. I would dare. But the source of love is not first of all found in a relationship. We love because God first loved us (1 John 4:19).

Every Single's Fear: 1 Corinthians 7

The most-quoted text about singleness in the church is without a doubt 1 Corinthians 7. The gist of this chapter: it is better not to marry. Because of this text, for a long time I bitterly disliked Paul. He seemed to be a boring and unfeeling man, purely motivated by reason and completely out of touch with his desires. But I think that I have done Paul a disservice, even though I still ask myself what kind of man he was. I hope to speak with him one day.

Before beginning this chapter, you have to consider the context in which Paul was writing. There were a number of things happening, the most important of which was the commonly held thought that Christ would return in a matter of years rather than a matter of centuries. In 1 Corinthians 7:29-31 Paul writes, "This is what I mean, brothers: the appointed time has grown very short. From now on, let those who have wives, live as though they had none...for the present form of this world is passing away." Living with the thought that it will all be over soon will definitely change your focus. Marriage, dating, and everything that goes with it belongs to this world, under the category "earthly affairs." They are of minor importance, especially when the world is on the brink of heavenly events.

Furthermore, Paul may see the growing persecution against Christians. In that time, persecution against Christians was yet to happen, but they were often bullied. But it would explain why he writes, "But if you do marry, you have not sinned, and if a betrothed woman marries, she has not sinned. Yet those who marry will have worldly troubles, and I would spare you that" (1 Corinthians 7:28).

Another reason was that Christians were few and far between, and the chance that you would find a Christian partner was slim. There were many less fish in the sea then than there are now. Moreover, many people were already married to an unbelieving partner who maybe questioned their beliefs. Either way, it caused problems. They wanted to divorce their partner because they wouldn't convert, or they felt guilty because they couldn't convince their partner to believe in the Jesus that they had so recently placed their faith.

Not marrying was absolutely not an option. You had to marry, otherwise something was seriously wrong with you. This way of thinking came from Jewish tradition. Every Jew had the duty to procreate in order for the Messiah to come. If you were a woman, you had no rights at all: no right to vote, no personhood of your own. You were your father's until you were your husband's. And of course you couldn't stay with your father forever. Therefore marriage, and definitely children, were your top priority, your only identity. If those didn't work out then you were looked down upon, devalued. But after Jesus came, everything changed; people were set free even from the long held 'duty' to marry and have children. Since then, you've been free to choose to be married or remain unmarried.

Sexual Faithfulness

Corinth was a Greek port city and the capital of the Roman province Achaea. The sexual morality in that time was abnormally licentious. This kind of sexuality wasn't just a possible lifestyle, but the norm. The people who decided to follow Jesus weren't then only making a choice for one God, but were making a choice to go against the culture in which they lived.

It's no wonder that there were questions about how to deal with fidelity within marriage. Paul takes the bull by the horns and writes about this topic, a commendable move. How many churches tend to cover this subject just once per year, max, out of a sense of duty?

Paul then writes that it is good that man and woman can experience sexuality within the context of marriage. He is incredibly clear about this, and quite countercultural. "A husband must give a wife what is due to her, and a wife to her husband." Immediately the focus becomes the wellbeing of the other. Timothy Keller explains this as the essence of marriage: pursuing the good of the other, apart from your self-centredness.

Paul was probably asked by the church in Corinth of how to deal with adultery that had occurred within the congregation. Paul begins his answer to the question without separating the question from the commandment. This is not his commandment, but God's. Matthew 19:6 reads, "What therefore God has joined together, let not man separate." According to the Bible, adultery is the only legitimate reason for divorce. Jesus says in Matthew 19:8 that divorce is only allowed because "of your hardness of heart. But," he continues, "...from the beginning it was not so."

What's even more interesting is Jesus' answer to the disciples. "If this is the situation between a husband and wife, it is better not to marry" (Math 19:10). Jesus rejects this! 'It was not that way from the beginning'. He refers to how marriage was created. It was created good. What He's referring to is that even in the case of adultery, healing within a marriage is possible and worth striving for. And that is a ground-breaking message, even in our society today.

Paul later recalls the much-cited Matthew 19:12: "For there are eunuchs who have been so from birth, and there are eunuchs who have been made eunuchs by men, and there are eunuchs who have made themselves eunuchs for the sake of the kingdom of heaven. Let the one who is able to receive this receive it." Often the text is explained in this way: There are people who don't marry because of physical/emotional reasons, something that occurred from birth. Think about disabled people, either mentally or physically. There are also people who never marry because they have been seriously disabled in the course of their lives; for example someone who has been emotionally traumatized in an earlier relationship or relationships. And there are those who choose to live entirely celibate lives.[16]

Jesus himself belonged to that last category. There was no other way; how could he do his work if he had a wife and children to support? It was necessary to choose a celibate life to accomplish his mission. There's nothing written about this choice, but it's possible that this was a part of his process in the desert. To live celibately was not his goal, it was more of the consequence of his goal to rescue us and restore our connection with God. Paul also made his choice to be unmarried in this way; not as a goal in of itself, but as a necessary choice in surrendering his life to God and working for his kingdom.

Paul never says, *It's an easy choice that will make you happy. That's* not what it's about. What matters is that you're obedient to the God who calls you. That you know who He is, and that you know who He thinks you are. Which is, loved. When in doubt, try this, say out loud: 'I agree with God about who I am'. And 'I agree with God about who He is'.

Dating Unbelievers

Paul continues writing in 1 Corinthians 7:12 that if you're married to an unbeliever or to someone who no longer believes, and the person wants to stay married, then don't divorce. Here too, you get the sense that Paul is giving advice to specific people and specific situations within this particular congregation. In this time people were coming to faith through contact with other Christians, so it regularly happened that one came to faith while the other did not (yet) believe.

When I look around, I often see the exact opposite happening. Friends who were both believers when they married, or at least actively going to a church, conclude a few years later that actually one or both of them no longer believe or don't want to continue "doing church." "Don't divorce," says Paul, unless "the unbelieving partner" wants to. But also remember that you have been called to "live peacefully." So if belief is a source of constant conflict within your marriage, remember what you are called to, especially if you, as the believing partner, are the instigator of these disagreements.

Dating an unbeliever if they cross your path, is no problem. You can do this only if you're a strong Christian, fully rooted in God. Then you won't fall in love with an unbeliever. So you can date someone in the arena of "getting to know them," and maybe even show them something of God. If you lose your faith over a cup of coffee you were in trouble to begin with.

But just as I outlined in the previous chapter, one of the few, clear instructions given in the Bible is in the area of relationship formation: do not enter into an unequal union with someone who does not believe or believes differently than you. You can definitely be a strong Christian and show something of God's love to someone else, but the fact is that somewhere inside all of us is someone vulnerable to a person who likes us and finds us interesting. When this happens, steps can be quickly taken to form a relationship.

We do live and work in this world. If we're living as we're supposed to, we'll come regularly across people who are not believers, but who of course we like or even really like. What happens then? Abraham said to his servant, *Above all else, make sure you that you find someone with the same background as my son. In other words, don't go fishing in a sea full of unbelieving women. You'll certainly hook one quickly, but that's not the sort of woman I want for my son.*

My friend's mother calls us Christian singles "the ethnic minority." Her idea is that we should organize ourselves in groups of Christian singles, either through Christian dating websites or singles groups in the church, so that we can fish from a larger sea. But what *is* "the sea"? Is that "the church," and if so, which church, and how far outside the walls of your own church can you date? What does it say about somebody to say they are "church-going?" It's too much to go into detail here, because this is the decades' old question of question of scientists who have been trying to uncover the "something" within psychology and religion. How do you define a Christian? Can I (or do I want to) date someone who calls himself a Christian, but hasn't been to a church for quite some time?

For now I find it important to point out that in the process of dating, the subject of someone's life philosophy/worldview must and should come up in conversation before you decide to continue a serious relationship. As a believer, you have even more to discuss with a non-believer. How do you deal with prayer? Will you go to church alone? How will you deal with sex as a couple? Will you live together or get married? And how do you want to eventually raise your children? It is more convenient to marry a like-minded person, as all the relationship experts agree. Having more things in common, to agree upon, offers a greater chance of long-term happiness. And yes, like-minded people can often be found more often within a church than outside it.

A friend of mine belongs to a group of women whose boyfriends or husbands aren't that religious or not at all (as she puts it). She says, "If you want to get rid of your faith, you should marry an unbeliever. You should also marry an unbeliever if you want to become more aware of your need for prayer." In other words, you put your faith at stake when you marry an unbeliever. On the other hand, her experience is that you can also find yourself closer to God. But it's never easy, and there is no guarantee that the other one will convert or that you'll hold onto your faith.

Single in Paul's time

Paul had other things on his mind. In no part of his letters is the subject of dating mentioned. He continues his story with a remarkable section. The part up until 1 Corinthians 7:17 is about marriage, and from verse 25 on it's about singleness, but the part in between, at first glance, looks completely misplaced. In this middle section, Paul says, apparently tongue-in-cheek, something about the circumcised and uncircumcised, the slave and the free, and how God values each equally. He introduces it with the words, "Only let each person lead the life that the Lord has assigned to him, and to which God has called him. This is my rule in all the churches" (verse 17). That is also the core message of this section.

Whatever your status is, you're good enough for God. Try looking at yourself through his eyes. It's not about ethical questions like whether to be baptized, a vegetarian, or giving ten percent of your income to a good cause. It's not about your status in this life, but about your heart.

Paul takes this quite far. In verse 21 he says, "Were you a bondservant when called? Do not be concerned about it. (But if you can gain your freedom, avail yourself of the opportunity.)" I can imagine that the servants who came to faith in Christ at this time wanted to see their freedom in Christ transformed into personal freedom. Completely understandable, but probably not always feasible. They had a social 'duty,' whether right or wrong, a calling to continue performing their work as well as they could so they could be a witness for Christ in the place they found themselves in.

This seems rather complex to me. Being a servant, working hard without being paid for your troubles, never being able to choose how to spend your time and energy, never able to make your own choices at all, let alone that no one cares, is almost unimaginable to us in the west. And to be able to see it as a place where God has called you! Paul does say that you shouldn't strive to remain a slave if you are offered an alternative. Regardless, Paul's main message is that even as a slave, you are completely worthy of God himself.

In the first churches, slaves often complained that God did not deliver them out of their situation. Today singles complain quite a bit that they still haven't found a partner, failing to realize the importance of living in the here and now. They forget that they're loved and valuable, even without being married. They don't always need to be happy about it, but they need to learn to live life-as-it-is-now as fully as possible, without believing that life begins with marriage.

The Choice Not to Marry

We keep reading. In 1 Corinthians 7:7 Paul writes, "I wish that all were as I myself am [single]. But each has his own gift from God, one of one kind and one of another." The "gift of singleness" reference that as a single you're beaten over the head with comes from here. Recently I found a website referencing a book with the hilarious title, *If Singleness is a Gift, What is the Return Policy?* [17]

Writer and theologian John Stott, who passed away in 2011, never married. He wrote, 'the gift of singleness is more of a calling than a confirmation, even though God will be faithful to those He calls'[18]. In the spiritual gifts test that some churches use, tell people that you have "gift of singleness" during the time you are single. That seems a bit twisted to me. All of the other gifts are about personality traits and talents. Singleness is something essentially different. It is not a personality trait or a talent, but a given situation, but that's where the gifts-component stops. It is therefore not a gift, and not something that you have to be happy with.

Paul continues in verse 25, "Now concerning the betrothed, I have no command from the Lord, but I give my judgment as one who by the Lord's mercy is trustworthy." What a captivating sentence, one you don't read often in the Bible: I'm now going to give my opinion, but I think you can trust me on behalf of God. So Paul gives his opinion. He thinks that "in view of the present distress it is good for a person to remain as he is. Are you bound to a wife? Do not seek to be free. Are you free from a wife? Do not seek a wife"(26-27). Don't look for a wife, men. Don't look for a husband, women.

Here Paul is saying something incredibly revolutionary: You don't have to be married to count. That was an entirely new way of thinking for that time. We often turn it around and tell each other, "Paul says that it is better to stay unmarried." You can take this text and be incredibly satisfied with your existence as a single. That's fine. But that's not what Paul's saying! He does say, you may be countercultural. If the culture tells you that you have to marry because it's the norm, look to Jesus and ask what he gives as the norm. You're equally worthy to him, married or unmarried.

In our time, being countercultural means marrying rather than being single or somewhere in between partners all of the time. Deciding to marry and have sex with only one person for the rest of your life, that is weird nowadays. That's what it's like to be a revolutionary in the 21st Century!

Being countercultural in our time also means stopping our search for 'the one,' believing that you can grow and become 'the one' for each other and to embrace single life as it is here and now.

Your Own Responsibility

Sometimes I write Paul imaginary letters. *Dear Paul*, one begins. *We've got a bit of a situation here. About a third of our church members are single, if not more. Almost all of these people want to get married, and they all say "God will bring my husband or wife to me." When I ask, "How is God supposed to do this?" then they say, "If it's God's will, then he'll prompt him or her to call me." What do you think of this, Paul?*

In my imaginary correspondence, Paul would say something like this, *Now I'm going to have to write this in all caps: FOR HEAVEN'S SAKE CALM DOWN. If you want to get married, fine, get married, but pursue it yourself and don't spend your evening sitting on the couch and gazing at the ceiling. God takes you more seriously than you take yourself.*

Of course God wants to bless you if you decide to step into marriage. He wants us to invite him into the choices we're making, and we can trust in his guidance. But, as I mentioned earlier, we shouldn't wait around for somebody to call. The issue of God's providence and guidance verses our own responsibility will always partially remain a mystery. I don't know why I'm not yet married, and I don't know if that falls under the category of 'brokenness' or 'leading.' What I do know is that nothing in my life is outside of God, and that he makes everything, even things I choose myself, work together for good.

Paul then says in 1 Corinthians 7:39, "A wife is bound to her husband as long as he lives. But if her husband dies, she is free to be married to whom she wishes, only in the Lord." So Paul is saying that just as you're free *not to* marry, you are also free *to* marry. You may choose whomever you want, so long as you choose in connection with God. And so here emerges the idea that a marriage is best made up of two partners who have 'something' to do with God.

It is Better to Be Single

Paul states that married people are concerned with more earthly matters than unmarried people. What I often indeed hear from those around me, is how difficult it is to experience the same intimacy with God after marriage. At the same time I see more singles buried in 'earthly matters' than most of the married people I know. Singles often have busier social lives, going to parties and concerts and on vacation. They often fill in their lives more than married people do. Especially if married people begin to have children, they find themselves increasingly more preoccupied with the basics (eating, working, and sleeping) than with all of the fun and social extras.

There is nothing wrong with all of these activities per se, but I think that a single person must be just as careful as a married person to intentionally be still before God. And that's not always an easy choice. Sure, as a single person you come to God more often when you have a need (because he is the only one you dare to disturb when you're lying awake worrying at 2am), but as a single person you also are generally more concerned with relationships than married people are. You're trying out dating sites or singles events. You feel obligated to date or be on the lookout because, *c'mon, don't you want to get married*? I think the married ones among us are often kept from their quiet times with God because of practical matters. Mornings are not an option, because the kids wake up before the parents. Then there are nappies to change and crying children to be comforted. Evenings there's that thing to be done for church, finish the daily household chores, and finally the tired parents collapse into bed. As singles maybe we're less distracted by practical things, but it is our inner restlessness that causes us (unconsciously?) to look for distraction. No nappies to change, but a good career to pursue. No crying children, but as many friends to see as we can stuff into our schedules.

A nun once confessed in an interview that it's easier to be unmarried in a convent than it is in the outside world. To begin with, you live in a community, which is already less lonely. Even more importantly, you are free from constant sexual impulses. What she didn't say outright, but what I find important, is this difference: the nun chose to remain unmarried, she chose for celibacy. I've never chosen to be single.

Celibacy and sexual purity (also called chastity) are not the same. As a single you can choose to be abstinent, or abstaining from sex, without choosing for celibacy. You then choose to have sex in a certain context (within a marriage), while celibacy is a vow of life-long abstinence.[19] Moreover, a celibate life often begins with a conscious choice and a corresponding ritual of entry. In this sense, it can be compared to the choice to marry. Being single doesn't often begin as a conscious choice, that's just the difficulty. It is just there. And then one day you realize that you've been unmarried against your will for longer than you expected to be.

And then it gets exciting. Because according to the writers I respect so much: being single is the best! (As if they are in some sort of club with Paul.) In Rodney Clapp's book *Families at the Crossroads,* a chapter is dedicated to singles. It's called "The Superiority of Singleness" and it begins with the following words: 'The most reliable callings come from reflecting on a situation that is more or less opposed on us. A calling is almost always a way of accepting the situation that at first was considered a limitation'.

In other words, a calling (in this case to be single), can grow as someone learns how to handle the situation of being single, even when they first experienced it as a problem or limitation.

In some circumstances, Clapp argues, being single is better than being married. In her article "Singled Out by God for Good," Paige Benton states that singleness is not an inferior state of being. It is not a plan B, a for lack of other options'. If that would be the case, heaven would be a plan B for us, because no one is apparently married there.[20] So this is God's best for me, she says. And it might be that God's definition of what's best for me might look much different than my definition of what's best for me.

Questions to discuss

1. Everything is turned over on its head in the New Testament. Even the meaning of marriage is completed transformed from family planning being at the centre to God and His global family. How do you reflect on that?

2. What do you think about Paul actually saying: be countercultural?

3. What does it mean for you to be countercultural?

4. The fullness of life has come in Jesus, and our goal is no longer just this life on earth, but also the life hereafter. This makes singleness a valid option, instead of a disabled state of being. Do you agree?

5. Do you feel this is the view in church? And if not, what can you do to change that?

Part 3

Single in the Church: The Possibilities

Chapter 5
Themes to discuss in your church

Let us not be content to wait and see what will happen, but give us the determination to make the right things happen.

Peter Marshall

Introduction

After looking at the issues and myths singles face, now it's time to look at the possibilities singles within the church have. There are no perfect solutions, and one, lone golden standard is non-existent. This section is about collecting ideas of how singles in the church can change their status and how churches can deal with their single members differently, or better. At the centre of all proposed ideas is the desire to strengthen the connection between those who are single and those who are married. This last part also contains the same two central focuses that I've explained and outlined earlier in this book. The first is recognising that the desire of singles for a relationship is a good and God-given one. The second is that singles must be encouraged to take the initiative for their lives and the questions they're wrestling with. I've expanded these two points into a course I regularly teach in various forms and places. In this next chapter I explain the thoughts and rationale behind these practical ideas. Finally, the last chapter contains practical tips for the single as well as the church.

A Theology for Singles

When reflecting on singleness, two themes keep coming back. On the one hand many singles desiring a relationship are unable to transform this desire into action. On the other hand, the truth is that you are already complete in your singleness, and now is the time to embrace it, making the best of it as your current reality for now, and maybe for a longer time. Many churches seem to lose their way within this paradox, or so it seems. They teach one way or the other: they either encourage you to find a partner as quickly as possible, or to practice contentment by accepting your current situation.

Al Hsu, author of the book *The Single Issue* (an absolute must-read for singles as well as churches) says that we need a theology for singles.[1] What he means is this: we need an idea, theory, or philosophy for what being single means for Christians and how to interact with them, and also what God says about the subject. As a single you often hear that such a theology is still missing, or that the teaching of some is strange or even unbiblical. You hear this when prayers go up for "people who are sick, sad, lonely, and single." Apparently when you're single you're lumped together with the "sick, weak, and nauseous." Or when there's a teaching given in a church on the subject of "finding the one," you hear that "God has someone very special chosen just for you." This is troubling, to say the least. In fact, it can be damaging for those searching for *the one* not to find him or her, and therefore left to conclude that God does not love or care about them. Otherwise he would have given them *the one*.

In some cases the theology is off, but in some cases it's simply missing altogether. How often do you hear someone in the church speak on singleness? The topic with its associated challenges seems to be taboo in many churches, for both pastors and singles themselves. My friend's mother told me about a church member who lives nearby in her neighbourhood. She knew that the woman had been single for forty years or so. Lately she had noticed this woman crying often in the church service, and asked herself if maybe this woman found it difficult to be single. She gathered her courage and found a good moment to ask her, but the woman vehemently denied that anything was wrong. She was perfectly fine, thank you very much! Absolutely nothing wrong with being single. This is possible, but not truly logical, based upon my friend's mother's observations. It's possible this woman was ashamed of her feelings, or denied them for so long that she no longer knew how to express how she felt.

Many married people tell me that they are so happy with our project, as it helps them to ask singles questions and makes the topic of singleness approachable. They're encouraged to think about it, also because of my own openness. Many of my married friends have a number of single friends, and notice that it's nice to be able to just speak openly and honestly about the subject. Before they didn't dare broaching the subject, afraid of possibility upsetting or hurting someone.

The elements for a theology of singleness, like what Al Hsu proposed, are based upon the topics I've mentioned above. On the one hand there has to be room to recognise and validate the desire for a relationship, and on the other hand attention has to be given for how singles themselves can take responsibility for the problems they encounter. Whereas the current line of thinking often seems to swing between "singleness is to be pitied" and "it is better not to marry," as far as I'm concerned a new, better theology is needed, something along the lines of "singles are equal members of the body of Christ."

It goes beyond this. In our culture we like to put everything in nice, neat boxes so that we can make sense of the world. Everything should be possible. Paige Benton writes, 'Disrupted theology is an attempt to explain singleness away. To say 'as soon as you are content with only God, he will bring you a partner'. As if God's blessings can ever be deserved by our satisfaction. To say 'You are too picky'- as if God will be frustrated by our wobbly demands and needs us to be more open mind before he can do something. To say 'When single you can completely commit to the work of the Lord'. As if God needs emotional martyrs to do his work, for whom marriage cannot be an option. To say 'before you can marry someone fantastic God will have to make you into someone fantastic'. As if God only gives marriage to those who are satisfactorily redeemed'[2]. So we don't need to be able to rationalize everything. Sometimes it's just simply the way things are, without some sort of holy purpose.

A theology for singles can begin with their equality. Let's say that the foundation of relationship formation shifts from sexual attraction (the foundation according to our society) to friendship. Friendship is much more useful in measuring your long term happiness with someone. Friendship, Cloud agrees with Keller, is the best foundation for your relationship. If there's a friendship, you'll be fine, and maybe that friendship will become something more. Or, as Cloud says, 'that's when other aspects of the heart and another part of God given love can come into play'[3].

God as a Source of Love

Many churches leave their singles hanging there. Their stance is that singles need to solve this for themselves; we don't know what to do about it. And this is the answer the church often gives when they have the chance to give a much better answer than society gives. It is precisely in this unfulfilled longing the single person has for a partner that the church's longing for Christ's return becomes most visible.

Theologian and ethicist Stanley Hauerwas says the church should know better. Where being with someone in a relationship or marrying is glorified elsewhere, Christians need to realize that that's not what life is about. We are not called to have the best marriages, we are called to have the best communities, he states. Growing in your personhood therefore must be done independently of your relational status, says Hauerwas. Even though many people hold off on personal growth until they marry.

The foundation and source of love is God. There is no real love without God (1 John 4:19). God is love, a love expressed in relationships. God's love is more fully illustrated in marriage, and is most visible in the grace you show your partner when, once again, he leaves the washing in the machine, or when she, once again, complains about your Netflix picks. But God's love is also expressed in the love between a parent and child, in the love aunts or uncles have for their nieces and nephews, in friendships, or any relationships that enter into your life.

Often God's love is short-changed in churches who only use the marriage status as a reflection of God's love for his beloved. But God's love is much more colourful and diverse than just the love between husband and wife. If marriage was the only image of

God's love, then singles would never be able to understand his love fully. Which is fully untrue; in fact, singles are often better able to communicate and experience intimacy with God, often because they are more likely to fall back into the security of his love, than into the security of the people around them.

The Church as God's Family

For a long time my church has felt the need to have a singles' group, one that could solve the "single problem" within the church. I don't believe that instituting a singles' group is the answer to many of the questions and problems posed here. A singles' group can be a good means to provide a way for singles to connect, but in itself should never become the goal of the church. It should never be the only answer to the question of what to do with all the singles around. "We have a group for you; go check it out."

After all, there's no "married group" that exists for all the married people, is there? It's also not biblical. As a theologian friend of mine wrote me, "You're not a person, separate from 'the other,' but you always define yourself based upon the other." What does this mean for the church as a community? You're not separate from each other. You belong precisely in this context, in connection with the people around you. In this context, the church can have a healing role. If you come from a family that wasn't tight knit or warm, the church can be one for you. The role of "family" goes beyond the individual church members.

If something develops specifically for church members, it always focuses on specific questions about being married. In a similar manner, it is always best to set up singles' groups that are focused on a specific goal or focus. And, as far as I am concerned, these groups are only temporary. It's easy in a church to develop a club of people that hang on together for years without actually getting somewhere. Our dating course is specifically focused on singles who want to know more about dating, and it's temporary. It's not a permanent place for people to hang out and talk about their experiences, but action and goal-oriented.

The value of this course has been enormous for our church. People start out a bit depressed about the state of their singleness, but quickly develop a new enthusiasm and enjoyment when they begin to meet all sorts of people attending. Meanwhile, there are surprisingly many participants who have found their "second half." That's not the goal of the course, but it is a nice bonus. The goal is to help people develop an action plan for the time that they are single, as well as to open up and give words to their feelings and experiences.

Giving Words to Your Singleness

It's exactly because of the lack of proper theology that the subject of singleness is discussed so rarely within the church. A single person is restricted to complaining every now and again about being alone. Complaining as such is not wrong. There is an appropriately named book comprised mainly of lamentations in the Bible , and in the Psalms you come across many complaints. Complaining can be a way of making space for your position in life, for your pain and for your needs. Look at lawsuits, for example. If someone does wrong by you, you are able to sue that person so that justice can be done. But this also illustrates that complaining can be meaningful only if it is followed by an action.

Complaining from powerlessness, or from the role of victim, often becomes endless complaining.

There is a kind of enduring strength that comes from putting words to your feelings. Giving voice to what's happening inside of you is enormously worthwhile and powerful. I see the biggest effect of this course on people is that they find the words to describe where they are at, where they couldn't find the words before. When we begin the course people come with the question, "How in the world are you going to do a five-part course about dating?" When they leave, we often hear them say in passing, "When is the follow-up course?" Words appear to give freedom and relief.

Many singles tell me that the subject is taboo in their church, especially if the church is made up mostly of families. That's when it becomes difficult to give words to their experiences, because they're so different from the other members. They don't want to be pitied, so often they avoid the subject altogether, which leads to deep grief growing unconsciously through the years until they arrive at our course. What I often hear after the course ends is, "If only I had heard this years ago!"

Giving words to the topic works internally for singles themselves and externally for church members. When people come from small towns or cities where most of the church members are married, I often hear them saying that singles by definition must be unhappy. Others think that singles are really happy, leading hip, full, and busy lives, without having to worry about anything or anyone, able to take long, adventurous vacations and pursue their dream career. I find both generalizations difficult. On the one hand I feel obligated to radiate happiness, even when I don't feel happy, purely because I *should* be happy. I feel obliged to say, "Everything is going *great*."

Sometimes I catch myself studying the faces of my married friends who don't have children, searching for signs of real or pretend happiness. Do they feel the same sort of pressure? Are they holding off on having a family purposefully, or has it not yet happened? Are they ready to consider other options, and are they sad about it? Do they have the same pressure to put on a happy face, as if there's nothing wrong? Take a risk and ask how they are. Talk with one another and find the words to ask what you are already speculating in silence. If you want to know how I feel as a single person, just ask. If I don't feel like answering, I will let you know. But it's more likely that you'll connect with me about things that are important to me.

Awareness

A course or small group on dating are not your only options. In our church our goal was to mainly raise awareness of the relationships within the church, so that the group of singles was viewed by the leaders as equal members of the community. This is why we presented our course materials to the team of teaching pastors. We also asked them to use singles as examples when preaching, when previously only married people or families were mentioned. And not only examples that had to do with topics like sex and temptation, but also normal things like quiet time and dealing with finances. So the team agreed and this change has seemed to have a hugely positive effect.

It is impossible *not* to notice the singles in any church when you start paying attention to them. It's amazing that this group has been sort of invisible. Just like married people, this group needs to be asked about their actions and to be encouraged in their growth. Not because they are single, but because they are Christians.

Just as the success of a marriage between two people, singleness often can't be explained. In Timothy Keller's favourite words about marriage from Ephesians 5 he carefully explains, "This is a profound mystery."[4] The mystery of two people who love each other and share their whole lives, finding joy and fulfilment and being in love into their eighties, is often a much bigger mystery than someone who has remained single their entire life. Benton suggests that ego-centrism plays a large role with singles, just as it does with married people, and that we can be saved from it by living in close relationship with others. Relationships, in all forms, are where words are given to our behaviour.

Awareness must first come from singles themselves. Singles shouldn't expect that their (probably mostly married) existing church board or council will one day think, "Hey, we should be paying more attention to our single members." This doesn't often happen, or if it does, it is motivated by the attitude of taking care of those "poor singles." Then something is put into motion that's quite different than what you need or want. If that's not what you want, as a single, be proactive. Let them see and hear you.

Speak up about your needs, but also about where your strengths lie. Our initiative has been successful mostly because we started it ourselves, based on our own needs. The reaction from our elders was, "Fantastic. We would have never come up with this ourselves. We've all been married for quite some time, and we never realized that this was needed, let alone known how to meet these needs."

Change the Dating Culture

We wanted to promote awareness in people and within churches through our course. In addition to awareness, our second goal was to change the dating culture within the church. Following the structure of Cloud's book, we wanted to create a culture where it is normal to date, where dating is an acceptable pastime of church members; not an activity where everyone immediately has an opinion about or becomes the centre of church gossip.

If you're a Christian who goes on lots of dates, you can quickly be put into the category of 'heart-breaker' or 'player,' especially if you're considered a 'serious' dater. Of course, maybe this *is* about your future. But first it's about having a cup of coffee or a glass of wine with someone. What Cloud suggests is that when you're dating you know your (healthy) boundaries, which can make dating a normal activity that has nothing to do with being a 'player.'

It can be extremely annoying if you want to get to know someone from church, and the next Sunday you realize other church members are analyzing whether you're a good fit or not. And that they feel free to tell you that they are so happy for you to have gone on a date with that "nice new boy." Often married people forget how often they themselves met up with someone (whose name they don't remember anymore) for a cup of coffee once or twice. It was just a date!

So make sure that dating becomes normal within your church, as a part of being single. Then it will be treated as 'just a date.'

Why Men Don't Like Going to Church

For the first time in history there are more highly-educated women than highly-educated men in much of the western world. Of those that leave the church, singles comprise the largest group, especially heterosexual men and lesbian women. They often disappear unnoticed through the back door. They often don't come back. Maybe they're still considered members or regular attenders on paper, but they don't show up. I know many women who are in a relationship with a man who doesn't attend church. Sometimes these men don't come to church because they can't deal with the church any longer or don't believe. Sometimes they've never been in a church, but the women involved are tired of waiting for the often passive men within the church to make a move, and have found a man outside of the church.

Men don't love going to church, according to David Murrow in the appropriately-named *Why Men Hate Going to Church*. The result is that you see few single men older than twenty-five attending church. Some of the songs that we sing at church with lines such as "Jesus I am So in Love with You," make me uncomfortable. I think to myself, "Honestly, I'm not in love with you at all, I'm in love with other things." As if being in love would stand in the way of honouring the Almighty God. Often I hear my male heterosexual friends say that they don't like singing these songs. "I'm not gay, okay?" Apart from the gay question, men often feel less comfortable discussing their feelings, and so many songs sung at churches today are incredibly emotions-focused. How can men express their faith (which many experience rationally) with such words?

Another reason why men don't often like doing to church is the emphasis that's placed on relationships. Having to constantly be sweet and friendly to everyone can be difficult to many men on the one hand, on the other hand single guys are surprisingly rarely on the receiving end of such care and friendliness. They say they are avoided, looked upon suspiciously.

The lack of "man stuff" in a church doesn't help either. Fun, right? Sitting, singing, and being chatty with "your neighbour." But when is something exciting going to happen? Most of the social activities, like home groups, involve coffee and chit chat. A yearly picnic to strengthen the bonds of community (i.e. drinking coffee and chit chat), or an activity that involves going door to door to invite people to the yearly Christmas service (another chatty activity) are things that often come more naturally to women than to men.

In my opinion, it's a luxury to be able to focus on all of the separate groups within a church. I think that most churches can't afford to do this. I also don't think it's needed. I think that we're called to be the church of God together, his family. And just as in a normal family, there will be problems that keep arising and need to be addressed. But just like in a normal family it's our task to be able to articulate our struggles and constantly seek a way to connect with each other. What would help the guys most, they tell me over and over, is just to be connected, to feel more included, just as they are.

Making a Connection

For those of us living in big cities, we'll walk past hundreds of people a day without waving or making eye contact, in order to be on time to that speed-dating event in which we'll talk with twenty complete strangers for three minutes to decide if we want to enter into a serious relationship. Feels a bit wrong, but in a city it is often necessary. When I first lived in a big city as an eighteen-year-old, I greeted everyone I passed on my bicycle, just as I was used to doing when I lived in my small town. In the first two weeks I was proposed to three times, threatened with death, and was surprised by countless astonished looks. So I quickly learned. In fact, I have had to remind myself to greet my neighbours, because I have taught myself to not make contact with people as soon as I leave the building. So how am I supposed to meet someone "out there"?

A friend often tells how she has consciously broken this "no contact" rule in the last few years when she's in the supermarket. Instead of focusing on her shopping and then disappearing again, she's made a game out of walking calmly through the aisles and making eye contact with every man who seems interested in her. Not to get a date, but also *not* to avoid meeting someone new. When she comes to the checkout queue, she doesn't look for the shortest one, but joins the line in which the most attractive man is standing. She regularly ends up having a nice conversation, with plenty of eye contact. She says that her way of "looking around" has completely changed, is more relaxed.

The focus is the practice of making contact. Recently I read ten tips about how to make contact in the supermarket. Use a cart instead of a basket, and accidentally and gently bump into people. Success guaranteed. I still haven't tried it! But maybe you are brave enough.

Making contact with the people remains difficult in our western world, and especially in our cities. It's likely that we have larger networks than ever, but we're also less connected than ever. When I look around at my street, I see almost solely people who are living alone. As is the case in most big cities in Europe and

America. Clients in my practice who live in small towns sometimes complain about a lack of privacy. But with people like my neighbours on my mind, I wonder what's worse. A lack of privacy and seeing people you know all the time, or the deafening quiet of loneliness in the city. There is no one to see you, and therefore there is no one to care about how you feel.

As the church our super power can be the ability to connect with each other. In most churches an 'empty chair' stands between families and the single person. The rule seems to be, always keep an empty chair between your family and the next one. That can feel nice and spacious, unless the next family consists of one person. This is especially lonely in big communities where everyone seems to be paired up. As a single person I want someone to sit next to. If he or she happens to be a boyfriend, girlfriend, mother, or father doesn't matter that much. It should be within the church that we feel able to connect with one another, as children from one Father.

Questions to discuss

1. How many single men are in your church? Where are they?
2. How many boys are in your church growing up alongside the girls? Where will they be in 30 years time?
3. What do the teenage boys in your church need in order to stay?
4. This current society where singles are a growing group asks for a theology of singleness. What is yours?
5. Church is best place for singles; we're all complete in God. How do you reflect on this?
6. We can be a much more connected church, making God's love visible in all its forms and functions. How?

Chapter 6
Ten Practical Tips for Churches and Singles

'May the people who are single and connected to our church feel welcome and acknowledged in their singleness, but equally challenged in their dating life. May those who are involved in singles ministry be aware of the opportunities and possibilities for relationship formation and growth in singleness. May the leaders of this church be aware of the amount of singles under their roof and adjust their agenda's accordingly'.

Thinktank advisory document to Crossroads International Church Amsterdam, april 2010

Introduction

These tips are intended for two groups. The first is for singles, and the second is to equip church leaders and pastors with ideas. For optimal effectiveness, both groups can discuss these with each other. The best tips for singles I have come across can be found in my book specifically on dating, Dare to Date. I still have yet to find good tips for churches. Most of the books that I read have been written by fierce proponents of an active singles ministry, mostly from the U.S. where the church culture is much different from the European church culture, but I believe these tips can be helpful for all groups.

Tip #1: Pray for Singles, with Singles, as a Single

Praying helps. I was brought up with the idea that work helps. The saying 'pray and work' always tipped a bit more in favour of the latter, which certainly hasn't been to my disadvantage. (While I'm writing this, for example, my parents are bringing me apples, tea, and a warm hot water bottle for my feet...the very picture of love in action). I've learned a lot from this work mentality, and my church is now benefitting. In a church that's a bit more evangelical, and where the emphasis is often more on prayer, there are some hilarious scenarios than can arise. "Are you offering that course again? But haven't you already offered it three times? And you have a job too, right?" Um yes. Where I come from that's called perseverance.

But the saying 'pray and work' doesn't start with *pray* for nothing. For singles praying can mean praying for that one person you want to spend the rest of your life with. Wonderful. You can do this daily. It won't tire God, although you might get fed up. I'm sometimes reminded of Paul's words in 2 Corinthians 12:8-9: "Three times I pleaded with the Lord about this, that it should leave me. But he said to me, 'My grace is sufficient for you, for my power is made perfect in weakness.' Therefore I will boast all the more gladly of my weaknesses, so that the power of Christ may rest upon me."

This could be an argument for praying no more than three times for a partner and after that just letting it go. Perhaps for the person who is able to do this it gives rest, but most of the singles I know pray for a partner daily because they feel the need for a partner daily. There is nothing wrong with praying for a partner, and there's no limit on how often you can pray.

For a long time, based upon this passage I thought I should be praying that God would take away my desire for a relationship. After all, it's often a painful and awkward desire if it remains unfulfilled. In some churches people will tell you that God gives you exactly what you need when you need it and that you should be extremely satisfied with what you have in the present (which is why it is called the *present*). In my opinion, Paul's point in this text is that we all live by grace. You don't always receive what you pray for. Or you receive it later, or differently than you imagined. But that doesn't mean that you shouldn't keep praying. And in the meantime you may learn to live within the tension of longing for what you don't yet have, between God's kingdom that is on its way, and God's kingdom that has already arrived. And that you, in the waiting, are indeed able to enjoy and be thankful for what you do have.

Often people find themselves stuck when praying for a partner, but there is quite a bit to pray about. God promises us that his words are our lamp to our feet and a light for our path. You only need a light for the path when you are on the move. As you move through life, you can pray for God's wisdom, for example, the courage to speak to someone you like. Or for insight into your own issues that you encounter. You can also pray for God's closeness while in search for a partner.

Prayer groups for singles can also be very helpful. I know from different singles in my church that they have a lot to offer. A friend told me that one of her married friends consistently prayed for her to find a husband, because she really wanted to. For my friend, this was incredibly beautiful and supportive.

And then there's the 'public' prayer that happens at the wedding (ceremony), that also plays a role in a positive way for singles. The most embarrassing prayers are the ones in wedding services where the 'lonely singles' are prayed for, that even though they are alone may be 'understood and accepted.' Please pray instead that they may also be able to experience their own wedding ceremony some day, or that they may see what relationship stands in their way, and how to deal with it. It is not easy, I know. Personally, I think it's perfectly fine not to mention singles in the wedding service at all. As a single person, give this feedback to your minister. It's not always clear to him how to best pray when it comes to singles.

Our course is always supported by a prayer team, and it is unbelievable how powerful that is and how necessary, because there is always something that goes wrong, no matter how well we prepare. In my church we call that spiritual warfare. During the course, two people are constantly praying in view of the corridor. The encouragement that comes from a wink given by somebody you know has been praying is immense. If your church decides to form a singles group, in whatever form, begin and end your time together with prayer.

Tip #2: Be an Example in Your Marriage

Whether or not you're a single or married pastor, you set an example in how you handle this topic. For example, I think it's fantastic how our pastors talk about their marriages, that it's one of the most saving things in their lives, other than Jesus, of course. This helps me, in the sense that it gives space for my desire for marriage.

Other singles may need to hear that marriage is not 'the be all and end all.' That's why we include the 'Marriage Myth Busters' in our course. In this section, the myths we attribute to marriage are invalidated. Even that is an example. Show what the reality of marriage is like. One of the most helpful parts of group therapy for couples is the recognition they see in other couples. "You can't talk about your problems at church, " they say, "no one does." You keep up the pretence that everything's just fine, even though the essence of being the church together means sharing love and sorrow. Not only love, not only the Instagram-approved-everything's-great picture. No, love and sorrow.

My favourite examples are always the "how we met" stories. Ask a random married couple how they met and you will always get a story, whether you ask someone on the train or someone in the church or even the airplane. I always find it fascinating how endlessly different these stories can be. And surprisingly enough, the man often has a much different version than the woman, even though they were both experiencing the same moment. I think God enjoys bringing people together in new and different ways. In my eyes this reflects his boundless creativity.

Moreover these stories are often very sobering for singles. Most people say things like, "we were not each other's types at all," or "we didn't really like each other for months," or "we really got to know each other once we got married." A dose of good medicine for the wishy washy, Hollywood-indoctrinated singles like myself. These stories keep both feet on the ground.

Finally, there is also a severe need for positive stories about marriages outside the church. Especially in a society that's dominated by negative messages about this so-called obsolete and outdated institution, it's crucial to have a positive counter sound. That's why Timothy Keller's *The Meaning of Marriage* is such a blessing to read as a single. There's not just 'happily married' or 'bored lonely and single'. There's a lot of goodness in marriage, but there's also a lot of blood, sweat and tears, humbling experiences and small victories at a great price[5]. In other words, let's tell the whole story when talking about marriage. The good and the difficult, the beautiful and painful. Just as I try to tell the whole story of singleness in this book. So everyone can relate.

Tip #3: Offer Good and Solid Teaching

From the think tank we started at our church, came a whole series of ideas for singles. Our approach is now mainly focusing on giving good teaching about the topic. Personally, I think that the church should be involved in this, and not only for church members, but for society. Society has almost zero good teaching when it comes to entering into and maintaining relationships. The one message is often, *If it feels good, do it; and if doesn't feel good, don't.* There's usually something about communication, but if 'love' is gone, it's gone.

God is a God of relationship, and the message that comes from that is not to keep to ourselves, but to share with the rest of the world. As in the question posed in an article from [insert media source], "What do you do when your first attraction disappears?" Some counsellors call that 'the first real day of your marriage'. It doesn't mean you have chosen the wrong partner, it just means you have to grow as an individual and take responsibility for your frustrations. There's no need to panic! That's what people often do when the attraction disappears. They dissolve into a downward spiral of panic and anxiety about love lost. And they quit.

In my practice I often advise couples to stay together and work through their problems, no matter how hopeless the case may appear. You take yourself and your relational dynamics with you into the next relationship, resulting in a good chance that you'll look for the same type of partner. It's most likely that you will run into the same communication problems again. Work out what you need to in this relationship, especially when your infatuation has faded. A human body can produce love hormones for three years maximum, and after that something else has to take its place. This applies to every relationship, so also for the second or third relationship.

We often offer a marriage course and pre-marriage course in our churches. Every couples therapist will tell you that a good marriage begins with a dating relationship, and that a good dating relationship begins with two healthy singles.

So this makes a dating course of some sort a logical part of this series. Together as the church we all have a responsibility. The reality is that in most big European cities, more than half of the residents are single. If these are the people you hope to reach as a church, then you need to offer singles just as an important place within the church as families.

Tip #4: Base Your Church on Friendships and Broaden Your Definition of 'Family'

Don't draw your sense of worth and being loved from dates, but draw it from God, your friends and family. This gives you a stronger foundation on which to stand. In my church it's easy to do this, but in many churches the whole social life revolves around families, leaving singles feeling like the third wheel. Having a family is not accessible to everyone. The singles' group aside, what about those who come from broken families, or people who have experienced a divorce? What about people who are mentally disabled or have some serious psychological challenges?

In the New Testament you mainly hear about the church as God's family. Jesus was single. I think that he was seldom lonely, because he surrounded himself with a group of good friends with whom he could discuss misunderstandings and whom he could give clear boundaries to. He seems to have had much less contact with his own family, or at least we don't hear much about them. What if the church of today was to consider friendship the primary form of relationship? In many churches the family is placed at the top, and in the next level comes other forms of relationships such as friendships, colleagues, and other contacts. This keeps singles out! You belong then to the lower category, or at least it feels that way.

Personally, I take care to maintain a balance in my group of friends between married and unmarried people. I really need my married friends, to develop a realistic picture of marriage, to fall back on the pace and structure of family life, and to get perspective on my singleness and dating life from those that don't have to search anymore. I really need my single friends, to share the highs and lows of the single life. To not feel as though I am the last living single in my area. To do fun things with on weekends, especially Sunday afternoons (family time).

There are singles who do not have this kind of balance in their friendships. Some are surrounded only by married people, which causes great unhappiness. Not only do they feel like the exception, they *are* the exception. There are also those who surround themselves only with singles, which seems easier. Then you don't need to feel like an outsider, but there is also a risk that it will get too comfortable.

In our church it's difficult to make friends with married people because of the structure of our services. The first service begins early, too early for those who have done fun things the night before with your single friends or had a date, and the first service also includes children's church (which is not that interesting if you don't have children). You can play along, sure, but there are limits to even that. The second and third services begin much later, at a time that children have to move on from cutting and colouring to running around or not just sitting in a service or being cared for in a nursery, but taking naps or eating. So for these parents the second or third services aren't an option. And so the married and single church attenders pass each other like ships in the night.

How could this be different? It's fascinating how much time, energy, and thought the average church gives to the children's programme. Kids can't do it by themselves, so rightly things are organized for them. But as a single you can't avoid thinking occasionally, "Okay, so a large portion of my tithing goes to the children's programme, youth, Sunday school, and parenting programmes. How (I feel bad even saying it) does this benefit me?" This can also be distressing for singles, especially if you would love to have children of your own someday, and the years are flying by.

It is the church that should think of family as greater than those who live within the four walls of our home. Living together as God's family, not as a romantic ideal, but in ordinary daily life. You can put this idea into action as a single by inviting a particular family in your surroundings to become involved in your life as a single, or inviting them to involve you in their family life. So many children in our society can use another safe adult in their lives, and that's the way you as a single can care for children. It's not for no reason that when you go to an infant baptism or dedication that you stand as a community and say "yes" when asked to stand next to this particular family in the caring for and raising of their child. Christian living communities are also a beautiful example of this.

As the church we can do our part in these relationships, just as Jesus did when he gathered his friends around him. What a beautiful picture, that Jesus sought out his friends before he began his work. Still, friends aren't everything. Even Jesus needed regular time alone; think for example of his journey into the wilderness. Our first safe place must be in God the Father.

Tip #5: Give Both Solicited and Unsolicited Advice

This is a daring tip, as at least part two of the tip seems risky. I dislike unsolicited advice, and my work experience has taught me that people usually don't follow it. But I'm still going to give this tip. A friend of mine often tells the story of how his pastor came up to him one day and asked, "So, why are you still single?" Okay, so that's not really unsolicited advice, but it is a question that in my experience many married people don't easily ask the singles in the church. They're afraid to hurt someone. Or they think it will open a can of worms when they ask it. Still my advice remains: ask boldly! Ask what you're curious about. The other person can always tell you that he or she would rather not talk about it. Or maybe someone will retreat back into their shell with a "Everything's fine."

For this particular friend the question was ground-breaking. He had never had a meaningful conversation about singleness before, and he was twenty-eight. He had always just done his thing, secretly hoping he would meet somebody, like what had happened for his friends. For him, this question was a turning point. He didn't have an answer, so he began to investigate. His search led to reading books and doing his due diligence in dating. And after a good number of dates, and finally, two years down the road and some turning points later, he's found a girlfriend he's very happy with. And it started with a simple question.

Sought out advice works even better. A church or people in a church have many types of advice to offer. With our course, for example, we make use of married couples who serve as mentor couples. The couple can watch, advise, and help out the single in any way. Life is complicated enough, and you don't always need to go to counselling for a problem. It is much better if you can bring these sort of life questions to someone in your church.[6]

In my book Dare to Date I talk about gathering a team around you as a single person. This is a group of people around you who can think along with you while you date. These people could include your friends, your family, a mentor or a coach. These are people who encourage you if you need it, or reassure you. Most of all you know that your team is on your side. They've got your back. And when dating sometimes feels like battle (and sometimes it does), they are your band of brothers.

Tip #6: Dare to Date

Dare to date. But where to start? It begins with organizing things in order to meet more people: parties, events, gatherings. They should go hand-in-hand with healthy teaching about singleness and dating. There is a big need for these types of activities within my church. It can vary from rock climbing to barbecuing with a group on the beach. Do a volunteer project. There are big outings organized several times per year where groups of people are sent out to different addresses to paint, visit the elderly, or give out free hugs in the city centre. These are amazing chances to combine doing something good for someone else while getting to know new people.

Pairing up can lead to rewarding introductions. People who know each person well can come up with a good match. A friend of mine has a friend who introduced her friend to her husband's friend. For three years she had this feeling that her friend and his friend would make a good match. "To end the nagging," her friend told her, she went with it. Until he stopped by. As soon as she opened the door "within five minutes I knew that my friend was right."

For the more shy, introverted ones among us, planning a bit or even being directly set up by friends or family can help enormously. In our culture you have to be extroverted in order to be appreciated, says lawyer and consultant Susan Cain.[7] Introverted people aren't big fans of parties or large gatherings, where they're not usually at their best. So if you're standing with that person in the middle of a big party and not enjoying your conversation, given them a second chance. It could be they are distracted by all of the noise and stimulation, thereby giving you the wrong first impression.

What this means is this: do not always go with the first impression. Countless course participants have assured me that they know only need five minutes– no, five seconds, to know if this person is their type, or is 'it.' That they really, really do know if they should date someone or not. Part of this is true. Helen Fisher, an anthropologist who researches relational formation, confirms that certain types fit together better than other types. But if you always judge based upon the first five seconds, and never give someone fifteen minutes or even two dates of fifty minutes to get to know someone better, then you didn't really give it a chance. You could be right, but you never know. You don't have any proof. It's just like always ordering that one dish in your favourite restaurant. It's delicious, of course, but you have no idea how the other dishes taste. Maybe there's a chance that you'll find something else on the menu that tastes even better.

Another way to meet people is speed dating, a method devised by a New York rabbi. The same dynamics are at work. In two minutes you don't get further than the first impression. And then you have to decide! Deciding so quickly is difficult, but keep in mind that you don't have to decide for the rest of your life. What it's mostly about is if you want to go out for a coffee with the person across the table from you. I know of several good relationships that began with speed dating. So speed date only when you are prepared to tick every box of every person you talk to unless they have a criminal record (which they probably will not tell you in three minutes).

For the people who never date, or always date with the same type, the advice is this: step out of your comfort zone. For once in your life go a few months dating different types of people, just to see how it goes. Try speed dating, let yourself be set up on a blind date, do something. Afterwards you're allowed to be more choosy, but then you've tested to see if your prejudices were founded and the chance is greater that your intuition will serve you better, and more tuned into reality.

Tip #7: Involve the Men

Most churches have become more feminine. Men comprise maybe most of the 'higher,' leadership positions, but much of the volunteer work and administrative tasks are often done by women. The church has become soft, argues Murrow, with plenty of room for feminine values and spirit and too little room for masculine influence. And because men can't express this lack of space, they begin to disappear. This includes married men as well as single men. A married friend told me that her husband doesn't like the church at all. He is believes in God, but sitting in the church and singing sweet songs tends to make him grumpy.

This also played a role with one of the couples who I saw as a therapist. I asked about it. What was this man's problem with going to church, according to his wife? "I don't have a single problem with it," said this particular husband. "In fact, I think it's great that she has so much support for her faith." "Yes," his wife quipped, "but that's just the problem. He thinks it's fine for me, but I would love to experience it together." "But I don't have the same kind of relationship you have with God," her husband answered. "For me, God is number one," the woman assured me. "And then my family." "And what about your husband?" I asked. It was quiet for a minute. The man looked at the ground, and then hesitantly at his wife. "Yes, he's second place," she answered softly, avoiding his gaze. And then a little more loudly, "But isn't that the way it should be?"

This was what she was always taught in church. The wife was expressing how she thought it should be, but I didn't think it strange that this particular husband didn't understand fully. There's a reason men can often be jealous of Jesus or the church. The church as a whole is the bride of Christ, but individual believers are not. Your spouse will never be as perfect as Jesus.

Once I read an article about a young couple who were fighting. She had done something that differed from what they had agreed upon together, and he was angry. "Jesus would forgive me!" she cried. "But I'm not Jesus!" he yelled back. It's true that God loves us unconditionally. In this sense, he is 'the one.' But God is beyond our lists of priorities. And, for a lot of people, he is less specifically present in our daily lives. Especially as a single woman you have to be careful not to put God in the place of lover, because compared to God, no guy who comes along is going to be good enough. Which is exactly how some Christian men feel: not good enough.

This is also because many men lack a positive, affirming, and present father. As a result, they don't feel complete and often feel insecure. Even in society there doesn't seem to be always space for a man to be "just a man." Think of the emergence of the so-called "metrosexual" a few years ago. It appears that men have to become more and more feeling and caring. If these men grow to know the Father heart of God, [8] they can feel more confident in their masculinity, instead of looking at women for affirmation. Because in general, many women are looking for confirmation themselves, and aren't in a position to give it, or at least, for the right reasons.[9]

It is therefore a challenge for the church to find a balance between the masculine and the feminine. Let men be men in the church, without expecting them to endlessly adapt themselves to all kinds of differences or suddenly become interested in all of the fun, warm, social events. It should bother you when you notice the men disappearing and that all of the positions available have been filled up by women. There's probably something amiss. Organize men's weekends, activities geared to men, etc. Make sure that there are clear male role models. If you're a male pastor, make sure that you would be able to attend your own church, that it's not bearable just because you're the one standing at the pulpit.

Tip #8: Calm the Women

I hear from men that women are often difficult to approach. Or they exude "tough" or unapproachable, or they look so scared and shy that they're afraid to make eye contact. The first category can often look "angry." It's a dynamic that often appears in a marriage as well, as I've briefly explained in the first chapter of this book.

Many women who have been single for a longer time, often appear a bit "angry". They may not even be aware of it, because they say that they'd really like to find someone to share their lives with. They think that they exude different vibes than they do. Because many of them are sad and hurting on the inside they think that's what shows. But the tone in which they say they'd like a boyfriend or the way they approach men often comes across as aggressive. They even spook me sometimes with their bitter responses when I speak on these topics. So what does this do to the average single man?

These women are trying to seek contact, and I understand that. They say, "Christian men don't take initiative." I know they mean to say: 'I'd like Christian men to talk to me, I'd like to get to know them'. But I think *You're taking too much initiative, and not giving them a chance.* But I keep my mouth shut, because the last thing they need is more criticism.

Single Christian women are usually loaded down with criticism. I usually hear the ever-popular "You're being too critical," alongside "You have too many wishes, your list is too long, you want too much." It comes in all sorts of variations, but the message is the same: You are too much to handle, and that is how Christian women feel. Like too much to handle.

And this completes the picture. Men feel as if they're not enough, or not good enough, and women feel like too much. Too sensitive, too nagging, too searching, too desperate. So it's been since the Fall. We women do (too many) dumb things, men stand there looking, and keep silent.

In the course I sometimes advise women to surround themselves for a time with very affirming people. Especially if they've heard "You're too critical, too picky....etc." too often. Let the people around you on your dating team affirm you for three months and see what happens. I have seen so many women transform from hard, angry, hurting and sad women to happy, expressive, and clearly softer people, making them more approachable.

As a single woman in the church you often get the message that God can and should be enough for you. If he is 'the one,' what more could you want? I have often felt guilty because I didn't experience it in this way, and continued to long for a relationship. I felt like a bad witness. In one service I heard a forty-year-old single woman describe Jesus as her lover. I don't know what I thought, but I knew that I couldn't speak those same words, and if I was honest, the idea made me nauseous. Jesus as my lover? Did I want to be able to say that? And was I short-changing a great, holy, and sovereign God?

To return to the incident between my female client and her unbelieving husband: God is not number one. God is everything in everything. He is all-encompassing. We don't need to rank him, like we often do with people, to give him a position in our lives. Your husband and children, if you have them, are allowed to be number one. God will not be limited to a priority list.

I think it's wonderful that so many women draw strength from Jesus and his love for us, and I believe in its power. But I also think women should be aware of the pitfall of thinking that a human man will be ideal. Just like the pitfall of working hard for God, for dates, and for 'finding a relationship' can cause you to run far ahead of a man and rob him of his initiative.

So, dear ladies, fellow females, slow down! Stop pointing out all of those passive men and look at yourself to see what you can do to get rid of your own anger and hurt. Imagine being *inviting* to those guys. They aren't perfect, but you aren't either. They want to be known and loved just as much as you do. Get to know them as they are. Be complimentary and appreciate their efforts, even if they aren't a knight in shining armour.

Tip #9: Use Singles As an Example and Source of Inspiration

Just as with the course, I had my doubts in writing this book. It's truly vulnerable to give your opinion on a subject that is so close to the heart. But just like the course, I went for it, especially motivated by the fact that there is so little good information out there. I found over a hundred books about the subject (I have stopped counting), but none of these books described what I was looking for. Or they were books written by people who were married at twenty-one, or who have forgotten what libido is. They may have written fantastic, wise things, but that doesn't mean that you feel heard as a single person.

Other books that I have issues with are the books that are about "everything single." As if that's possible. The toughest category is always the books with all the answers. I don't pretend to have all of the answers, and maybe I even create more questions than answers. Yet I'm thankful now for my searching. However difficult I've found it at times, it's really wonderful that my search has been able to help others. This is confirmation to me that we as singles still have much to learn from one another.

And this example is also for singles themselves. For many people our course comes with recognition ("Oh, so you struggle with this too? Oh wait! You also don't know what to do with Christmas and your birthday and vacation?") and inspiration from others' examples. How do you handle dating? What do you tell someone when you don't want to date them anymore? How do you deal with loneliness and how do you give boundaries when the other person doesn't have them? You can learn quite a lot from your fellow singles. Giving this course and writing this book has taught me new things over and over again.

What a church can do is give the singles they know a place to tell their story. This is a powerful things. So many singles, so many stories, and for each one another person's take can be helpful. How I deal with my singleness is not the same as my neighbour deals with his, or my friend who lives in a small town. We're different people with different circumstances and different desires. But each of our stories have something meaningful, something powerful that tells us how God deals with us and reflects something of him and us back to us. Let singles have a chance to speak, to make their story known so that other singles no longer feel alone and have more words to use to share about what it's like to be single, the ups and downs, the positives and negatives.

As a church, look at what you can learn from your singles. Often singles have rich prayer lives and a strong connection with God, because they are more dependent on him. See how you can enrich each other's lives, instead of envying each other's privileges.

Tip #10: Create Connection. Go On an Adventure Together

Ultimately, it's about connecting with God, yourself, and the people around you. A church can play an important role here. If you don't have time or space to start a singles' group, fine, but make sure that your singles feel just as a part of church life as the married people and families within your congregation. Realize that they need to feel just as included as anyone else. And make sure that as a single you communicate what you need, instead of waiting for your church to attend to your needs.

Don't count on small groups to be your only source of connection, but go together on adventures, just like the first congregations did. Rethink the size of your church; the first congregations were small. Look at your shared mission, hopefully it was not written to keep all the groups satisfied, but to join together as a whole and make disciples of all nations. Nothing is as bonding as a common goal.

Make contact with each other, not only verbally but also physically. My church is good at giving hugs. Everyone needs touch. Make sure that there are times to eat together and do fun things. Stop with the gossiping. If people have a relationship worth sharing, they'll talk about it, or you'll see it on their Facebook status. Leave them alone until it's "public." Make it a normal thing for singles to get to know each other better, without being immediately labelled. And if people are seriously dating and then break up, let it happen. People can always change their minds.

Be practical, and invite each other over. Do this especially on commercially hyped days like Christmas, Easter, Thanksgiving, or just on ordinary weekdays. If you want, invite each other on vacation, or plan a fun camping trip with a group of people. Organize a singles' day in your church as an alternative for Mother's Day or Father's Day, a day that celebrates the positives of being single.

Above all I hope that this book is an inspiration for singles to set something up in their church or to communicate what they need to the church leadership. There are plenty of ideas, but it's important to find what fits your own church community the best. In the index you'll find a overview of our ideas in the think-tank, some of them which are in progress, the others more of a fun suggestion or created for inspiration. Be a community where people can get to know each other, where they can make real contact. This is not about fulfilling your own desires, but as a goal to connect with another. This alone would be such a radical and adventurous way of interacting that it's worth a try!

Questions to discuss

1. What matters is that you, as a church community, adventure through life together. How is this in your church?
2. Are you as a single person fully involved in the ups and downs of church life as other members, and vice versa?
3. How do you connect to God, yourself, your community and new single people you meet? Do you dare to date?
4. How do you feel about involving the men in your church? And how would you rate your church leaders for doing so?
5. How do you feel about calming the women in your church? And how would you rate your church leaders for doing so?
6. If there's one thing you could change about the dating culture in your church, what would it be, and how could that practically be achieved?

Epilogue

Reading through all this material now, sitting at my desk in a beautiful monastery in quiet Brecht, Belgium in October 2019 is such a special experience. I wrote this book when I was single and actively searching for meaning in my life and more meaningful dating. It is written straight from the heart and I admire the smart, witty and passionate single self I was.

Married now and two kids richer, I am happy to be standing at the other side of this quest for a mate. I am thankful that I've actually found someone to share my life with and I wouldn't want to go back. But the things I have learned and the way they have formed my personality and shaped my character are priceless. They are the wisdom I take with me on this journey of marriage and motherhood.

I've been in doubt over publishing this book in English so long after it has been published in Dutch. And sure enough, I've edited a few bits and pieces out and added a few others, but by and large it's still the same book. And I still see the same need for it, for my voice to be heard in churches when it comes to both defending singleness as a good and holy place to be in, and defending the quest for marriage through dating as a good and valuable adventure to undertake, also as a Christian single. I would phrase some things a bit milder now maybe, but I want my single voice to be heard as much as my married voice in these matters. So when speaking now I will do the more mellow version of what I have learned at the time, but when it comes to publishing this book I'm happy to hand to microphone once again to my former single self.

Here she is, in all of her vulnerability, passion and fire. Hoping to change the culture in order to change the world. To see Gods kingdom grow and grow and grow. Thank you for listening.

Praise for Dare to Date

Dare to Date is a brilliant book. It is thoughtful, honest and engaging. Based on Aukelien's professional and personal experience the book should be placed on the 'must read' list for anyone dating, considering dating or involved in supporting single people in the church. I have recommended it widely to people in our congregation and people universally love it. Buy it and read it."

> - *Jenny Peters - St Mary's Bryanston Square and Director of Connected Live, London, U.K.*

At Christian Connection we have been bringing single Christians together for over 16 years. But time and time again, we encounter Christians who are afraid, discouraged or uncertain on whether or how to date. Church life can often put great pressure and expectation on Christians but without offering help and support. Dare to Date really addresses these issues with wisdom, faith, insight, practicality and true stories.

> - *Jackie Elton, founder and MD of Christianconnection.com*

Aukelien brings years of experience counselling about relationships, as well as her own experiences of dating, to help people to find a new and better way forward. . . [she] offers invaluable advice on how to date well, how to widen the pool of potential marriage partners and how to explore the possibility of a longer-term relationship.

> - *Rev dr. Nicky and Sila Lee, Relationships Central HTB London, U.K.*

After attending a special event at St Mary's in Marylebone in London, with Aukelien as the headline guest I was moved to buy the book and learn more. I learnt a lot about myself and dating and now am in a happy year long relationship. Still growing and learning, but this book dared me to open my mind and heart.

- *Abi*

I have read many different books on Christian dating and this was the first that made sense to me. It really helps that the author comes from a place of 'knowing' what it's like to be a single in the church, rather than just guessing what it's like. Having come to a place of disappointment with the lack of men in the church (which she also addresses) this book gave me the encouragement to get back into dating. There are parts I found challenging, particularly having to address some of my own myths about Christian dating, but overall it has brought nothing but positivity. After reading this book I have been on three dates already and I am much more open minded now about finding love. Thank you!

- *Amazon customer*

An amazing read. And challenging. I did also take the course and after many years of singleness I changed my approach to dating. Successfully I add as I got married within the year, at age 39!!

- *MaddyChristine HB, U.S.A.*

This is an excellent book full of practical advice, challenges and examples. Van Abbema brings a reality to the assumptions about dating while also holding in balance the expectation that to love God first is possible. Read this, recommend this, pass it on.

- *Pheebs*

Aukelien is a force. As a therapist and speaker, she dares to take on this sensitive topic of dating, naming what threatens our ability to connect with each other, and challenging us to do something about it. This book is not only about dating, but about healthier relationships: with God, with others, and with yourself.

- *Erin Hobbie, Florida, U.S.A.*

Additional Reading

My work

For over ten years now I've been speaking on all things single and dating in church. I've written many blogs in two languages, which have been published on various platforms. I've also filmed a Datingcourse, available on YouTube. To find out more about my ministry and work with singles and for singles go to aukelienvanabbema.nl, and follow me on Facebook, Instagram or YouTube.

Singlefriendly Church

Singlefriendly church is a brilliant resource for both singles and church leaders when it comes to stats, material and topics to discuss regarding singleness. Go to singlefriendlychurch.com

Pray for a mate

Another great set of resources that I only discovered after writing this book unfortunately, is provided by Kris Swiatocho, Director of www.TheSinglesNetwork.org Ministries. Kris is an international speaker and author who focuses mainly on teaching how to reach, grow and minister to single adults. One of her books is: Everyone Knows a Single Adult; The FAQ's of Singles Ministry. It has over 50 experts in the field of singles ministry answering 100 questions about singles and young adult ministry.

Books On Singleness

Kate Wharton, *Single Minded.* Lion Hudson, U.K. 2013.
Sam Allberry, *7 myths on singleness*. Crossway books, U.K. 2019.
Al Hsu, *The single issue*. IVP, U.K., 1997.

Books On Relationships and Dating

Aukelien van Abbema, *Dare to Date.* SPCK, London, U.K. 2017.

Timothy Keller, *The Meaning of Marriage*. Dutton, New York, U.S.A 2011.

Henry Cloud, *How To Get a Date Worth Keeping.* Zondervan, U.S.A. 2005.

Notes

Introduction

[1] Officially my First book was Single in Church, published in Dutch in 2012. Dare to Date followed in the year after, also in Dutch, to be published in 2017 in English. And in 2018 in Hungarian, to be complete. That's not too confusing, right?

Chapter 1

[2] in the Dutch newspaper *the Parool* (February 11, 2012)

[3] https://ec.europa.eu/eurostat/statistics-explained/index.php/People_in_the_EU_-_statistics_on_household_and_family_structures#Single-person_households

[4] How to get a date worth keeping, Henry Cloud

[5] My book Dare to Date, published in 2017 by SPCK, is the 'What and how', this book Single in Church is more of the 'Why?'

[6] Mahoney, E.R. (1980). Religiosity and Sexual Behavior Among Heterosexual College Students. *The Journal of Sex Research, 16,* 97-113.

[7] More on this dynamics in Sue Johnsons excellent book 'Hold me tight'.

[8] The single issue, Al Hsu

[9] As read in 'A good man is hard to find: unless you ask God to be head of your search committee', Jo Lynne Pool (tip: you don't need to read this)

[10] The Datingcourse is a term we first used in Crossroads in 2008 as opposed to the Marriage course and the Parenting course, or rather, in addition to those courses, as they were already available in our church. I now teach this course in various forms, online on my YouTube channel (Aukelien van Abbema) or in

churches and at conferences. More information and a bookingform can be found on my website www.aukelienvanabbema.nl

[11] Dare to Date, Aukelien van Abbema (2017, SPCK).

[12] Singled out by God for good, Paige Benton in PCPC witness, feb. 1998 in PCPC Witness (www.pcpc.org)

[13] No. The best guys come to our course. I met my husband there.

Chapter 2

[1] More information can be found on singlefriendlychurch.com, research done by David Pullinger.

[2] Centraal Bureau voor de Statistiek (CBS) – Dutch census

[3] Daten is meten, Droge&Sel (To date is to know)

[4] CBS, 'Het heilzame huwelijk' (The wholly marriage)

[5] Elsevier, 11 februari 2012, Gezond, rijk en gelukkig, met dank aan het huwelijk, José van der Sman. (Happy, rich and healthy thanks to marriage).

[6] http://www.laughyourway.com/blog/soul-mates-and-selfishness Mark Gungor

[7] Psychology Today, jan/feb 2012, p. 59

[8] Lewis as quoted in 'The Meaning of Marriage', Tim Keller

[9] Which is what I ended up doing, in case you're wondering. No regrets. Loads of grace and a wonderfully wise boyfriend needed.

[10] For more on this, see Dare to Date.

[11] Eldredge, Captivating p. ix (2005).

[12] Holy Longing, Lisa Graham McMinn

Chapter 3

[13] Shaunti Feldhahn's book *For Women Only* is a good place to start. You might also want to check out John Gray's book *Mars and Venus* or his book specifically for singles, *Mars and Venus On a Date*.

[14] Idem

[15] I am aware of not addressing same sex attraction here and using rather stereotype gender roles. This is a convenience thing and to address the majority of my readers, not to form a judgment or state how things should be.

Chapter 4

[16] Singles in the bible, David M. Hoffeditz
[17] "If Singleness is a Gift, What is the Return Policy?" Holly Virden en Michelle McKinney Hammond
[18] *The Single Issue*, Al Hsu, p. 178.
[19] For a more detailed discussion about this, read *Real Sex* by Lauren F. Winner.
[20] "Singled Out by God for Good," Paige Benton

Chapter 5

[1] In Al Hsu's book *The Single Issue*.
[2] In Paige Benton's article "Singled Out by God for Good."
[3] *How To Get a Date Worth Keeping*, Henry Cloud, p. 218.
[4] *The Meaning of Marriage*, Timothy Keller

Chapter 6

[5] *The Meaning of Marriage*, Timothy Keller, p. 21.
[6] Also see Larry Crabb's book, *Connecting*
[7] "Just be Quiet," Sarah Korones, *Psychology Today* Jan/Feb 2012.
[8] Highly recommended reads include Mark Stibbe's *I Am Your Father* and *The Father You've Been Waiting For* as well as *The Prodigal God* by Timothy Keller.
[9] *Wild at Heart,* John Eldredge

Printed in Great Britain
by Amazon